The World from 1000 BCE to 300 CE

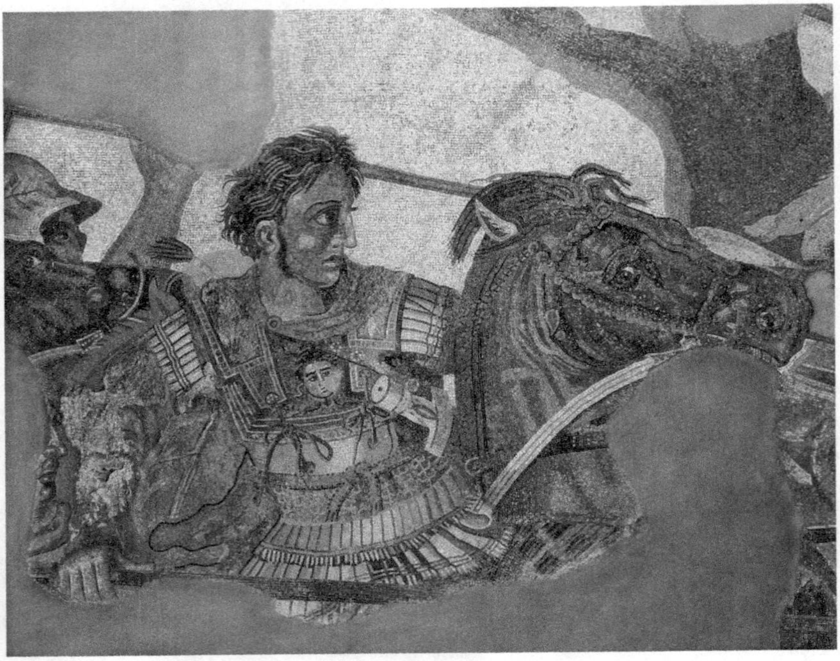

The
New
Oxford
World
History

The World from 1000 BCE to 300 CE

Stanley M. Burstein

OXFORD
UNIVERSITY PRESS

OXFORD
UNIVERSITY PRESS

Oxford University Press is a department of the University of Oxford. It furthers the University's objective of excellence in research, scholarship, and education by publishing worldwide. Oxford is a registered trade mark of Oxford University Press in the UK and certain other countries.

Published in the United States of America by Oxford University Press
198 Madison Avenue, New York, NY 10016, United States of America.

© Oxford University Press 2017

All rights reserved. No part of this publication may be reproduced, stored in a retrieval system, or transmitted, in any form or by any means, without the prior permission in writing of Oxford University Press, or as expressly permitted by law, by license, or under terms agreed with the appropriate reproduction rights organization. Inquiries concerning reproduction outside the scope of the above should be sent to the Rights Department, Oxford University Press, at the address above.

You must not circulate this work in any other form
and you must impose this same condition on any acquirer.

CIP data is on file with the Library of Congress
ISBN 9780199336142 (Hbk)
ISBN 9780199336135 (Pbk)

Frontispiece: Mosaic from Pompeii depicting Alexander the Great's victory at the Battle of Issus. Shutterstock 229537219

For my teachers, who showed me how to do it

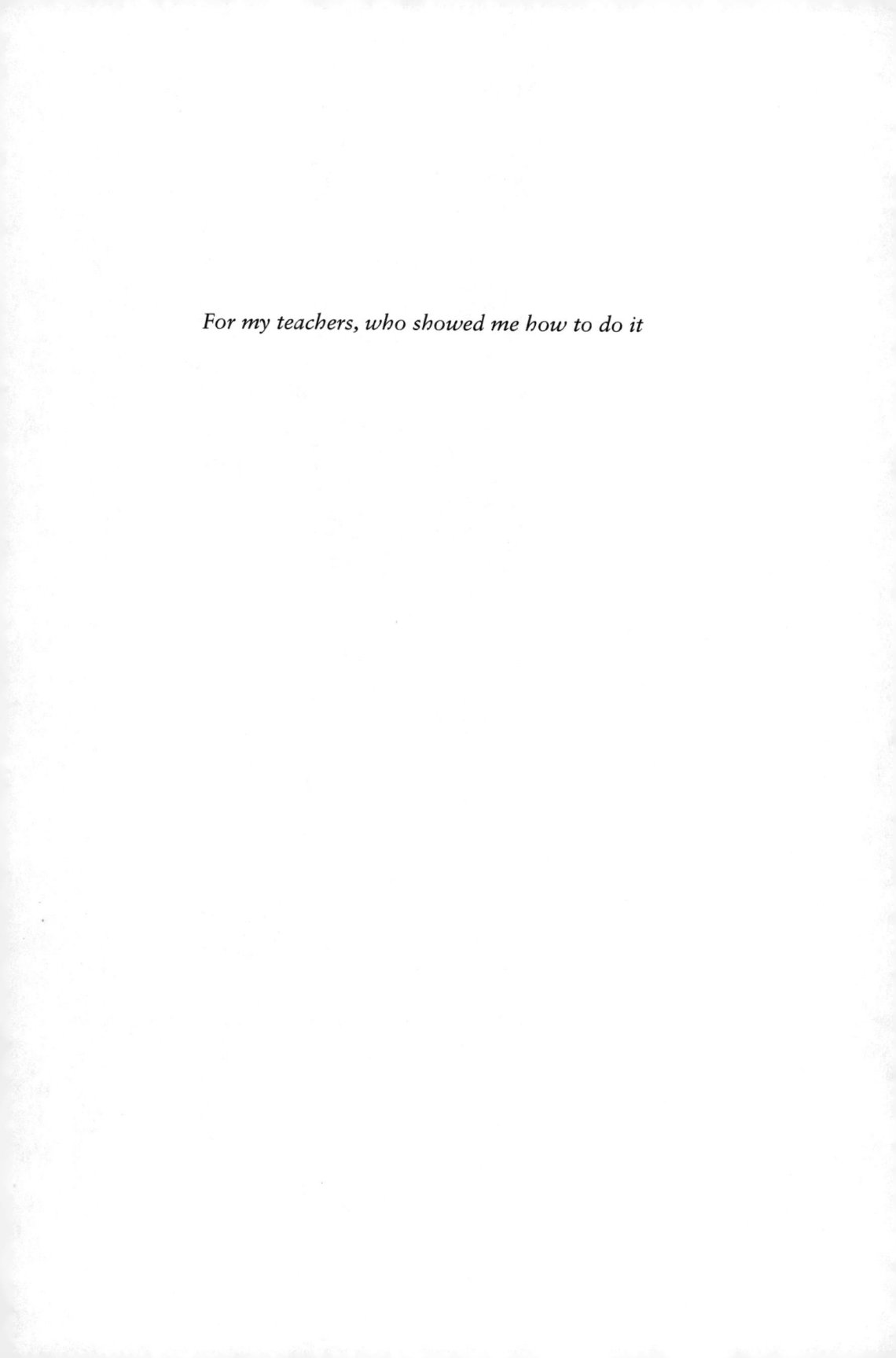

Contents

Editors' Preface ix

Preface xi

CHAPTER 1 The New World of the Early First Millennium BCE (ca. Twelfth–Eleventh Centuries BCE) 1

CHAPTER 2 The Early Iron Age (ca. Tenth–Seventh Centuries BCE) 16

CHAPTER 3 East Meets West: The Rise of Persia (ca. Sixth–Fifth Centuries BCE) 35

CHAPTER 4 The New World of the Macedonian Kingdoms (ca. Fourth–Second Centuries BCE) 53

CHAPTER 5 The Rise of the Peripheries: Rome and China (ca. Third–Second Centuries BCE) 71

CHAPTER 6 A New Order in Afro-Eurasia (ca. Second Century BCE–Second Century CE) 87

CHAPTER 7 Crisis and Recovery (Third Century CE) 106

Chronology 125

Notes 127

Further Reading 131

Websites 137

Acknowledgments 139

Index 145

Editors' Preface

This book is part of the New Oxford World History, an innovative series that offers readers an informed, lively, and up-to-date history of the world and its people that represents a significant change from the "old" world history. Only a few years ago, world history generally amounted to a history of the West—Europe and the United States—with small amounts of information from the rest of the world. Some versions of the "old" world history drew attention to every part of the world *except* Europe and the United States. Readers of that kind of world history could get the impression that somehow the rest of the world was made up of exotic people who had strange customs and spoke difficult languages. Still another kind of "old" world history presented the story of areas or peoples of the world by focusing primarily on the achievements of great civilizations. One learned of great buildings, influential world religions, and mighty rulers but little of ordinary people or more general economic and social patterns. Interactions among the world's peoples were often told from only one perspective.

This series tells world history differently. First, it is comprehensive, covering all countries and regions of the world and investigating the total human experience—even those of so-called peoples without histories living far from the great civilizations. "New" world historians thus share in common an interest in all of human history, even going back millions of years before there were written human records. A few "new" world histories even extend their focus to the entire universe, a "big history" perspective that dramatically shifts the beginning of the story back to the Big Bang. Some see the "new" global framework of world history today as viewing the world from the vantage point of the moon, as one scholar put it. We agree. But we also want to take a close-up view, analyzing and reconstructing the significant experiences of all of humanity.

This is not to say that everything that has happened everywhere and in all time periods can be recovered or is worth knowing, but that there is much to be gained by considering both the separate and interrelated stories of different societies and cultures. Making these connections is still another crucial ingredient of the "new" world history. It emphasizes connectedness and interactions of all kinds—cultural, economic, political, religious, and social—involving peoples, places, and processes. It makes comparisons and finds similarities. Emphasizing both the comparisons and interactions is critical to developing a global framework that can deepen and broaden historical understanding, whether the focus is on a specific country or region or on the whole world.

The rise of the new world history as a discipline comes at an opportune time. The interest in world history in schools and among the general public is vast. We travel to one another's nations, converse and work with people around the world, and are changed by global events. War and peace affect populations worldwide, as do economic conditions and the state of our environment, communications, and health and medicine. The New Oxford World History presents local histories in a global context and gives an overview of world events seen through the eyes of ordinary people. This combination of the local and the global further defines the new world history. Understanding the workings of global and local conditions in the past gives us tools for examining our own world and for envisioning the interconnected future that is in the making.

Bonnie G. Smith
Anand Yang

Preface

In a striking passage of the *Kephalaia*, a collection of the statements of the third-century CE religious leader Mani,[1] that was compiled sometime after the middle of the third century CE, Mani claimed, "There are four great kingdoms in the world. The first is the kingdom of the land of Babylon and of Persia. The second is the kingdom of the Romans. The third is the kingdom of the Axumites. The fourth is the kingdom of Silis [that is, China]. These four great kingdoms exist in the world; there is none that surpasses them." Mani was describing the result of a revolutionary change in the political and cultural life of Afro-Eurasia. In 1000 BCE numerous regional states, both small and large, structured the life of the eastern hemisphere. By 300 CE, however, they had largely been replaced by a small number of great empires that were home to cultural traditions based on canonical texts, a core group of authoritative works that formed the basis of elite education. That remarkable transformation is the subject of this book.

The story begins with the collapse shortly before 1000 BCE of the regional empires that had dominated the Near and Middle East and east Asia during the second millennium BCE and the opening of a period of intense regionalism, widespread population movements, and virtually chronic warfare throughout Afro-Eurasia. Almost simultaneously, the creation of the world's first effective cavalry by the nomads of the central Asian steppe made possible a new form of empire: tribal confederations led by charismatic leaders and covering huge territories. Interaction between the empires of the steppe and those of the temperate zones was one of the main drivers of political, cultural, and economic development in Afro-Eurasia until the emergence of the political order described by Mani around 300 CE. In the process, the regionalism that had characterized the early first millennium BCE disappeared. In its place, from the Atlantic to the Pacific a handful of great empires—Rome, Sassanid Persia, and the Jin Empire in China—ruled more than half of Afro-Eurasia's population.

Despite their individual peculiarities, these empires were remarkably similar in their basic structures. Economically, all were based on agriculture supported by extensive coinage systems, iron technology, and substantial internal communication systems: roads and maritime routes in the Roman west, roads in Persia, and roads and canals in China. Socially, they were significantly more complex than their predecessors in the second millennium BCE, being characterized by increased urbanization, the proliferation of new social and economic roles including professional writers and artists and philosophers and scientists, limited freedom from traditional gender roles for a handful of elite women such as the Chinese historian Ban Zhao, and growing importance of various forms of dependent and un-free labor. Governmentally, all were autocratic monarchies, whose rulers claimed to rule by divine right but whose actual authority rested on the support of standing armies and extensive bureaucracies staffed by officials whose education was based on the "canonical texts."

These states were not isolated from one another. By the early centuries CE, increasing connections among these empires had made this period the world's first global era. Trade routes both by land such as the central Asian Silk Roads and by sea through the South China Sea and Indian Ocean connected the great Afro-Eurasian empires to each other and to lesser states in the southeastern and southern parts of Asia, southern Arabia, northeast and east Africa, and the Sahara and the Sahel (the belt of dry grassland immediately south of the Sahara) with significant cultural effects. Asian foods including cinnamon, chicken, pepper, and rice became dietetic staples in the Near East and Mediterranean; bananas from Indonesia were beginning to transform life far into the interior of Africa; and Mediterranean glass and ceramic goods and wine became desired throughout northeast Africa, southern Arabia, and south and southeast Asia.

Religions also followed the trade routes. Buddhism, for example, spread north from its Indian home through central Asia to China and south and east to Sri Lanka and southeast Asia, meeting along the way Western religious traditions—Christian, Gnostic, and Zoroastrian—and their artistic forms. This encounter gave birth to a new religion, Manichaeism, which would have a long future in the Middle Ages, as well as new schools of art such as the Gandhara school of Buddhist art, which used Greco-Roman forms to provide the model for figural representation of the Buddha throughout central and east Asia.

Common enemies and common problems also led to common solutions throughout Afro-Eurasia. So, for example, the threat posed by the nomads of the Eurasian steppe to the new empires throughout the period led to similar policies: divide and conquer diplomacy, use of barriers to control the movement of nomads, and growing reliance on elite cavalry units to counter nomad raids. At the same time, to unify their diverse populations in the face of the threats from the steppe nomads, the two most exposed empires, Rome and Persia, adopted the model of official churches based on state-recognized scriptural canons, or religious doctrines. The first to appear was Zoroastrianism in third-century CE Persia and then a century later Christianity in the Roman Empire and its Armenian and Aksumite neighbors. Despite the many crises of the mid-first millennium CE, however, the connections established during the thirteen hundred years dealt with in this book persisted and formed the basis of social and economic life throughout much of Afro-Eurasia for the next millennium.

The regions discussed in this book constitute what Greek and Roman geographers called the *oecumene*, the inhabited world. The same geographers, however, also speculated that there were other *oecumene* besides the one occupied by themselves and their neighbors, and they were, of course, right. By the early fourth century CE there were still major regions of the world that had only barely been touched or were completely untouched by these developments. Most important among these regions were sub-Saharan Africa, the Americas, and Oceania. Although the extent of their separation from the core of Afro-Eurasia varied, they all had one thing in common. They followed independent paths to complex society.

Closest to the core of Afro-Eurasia was sub-Saharan Africa where iron-using, mixed-agricultural societies became increasingly common during the first millennium BCE and the first millennium CE. Cities that were centers of commerce also appeared in the inland delta of the Niger River in Africa. Not surprisingly, the separation of sub-Saharan Africa from the rest of Afro-Eurasia had begun to break down by the end of the first millennium BCE with the expansion of the Indian Ocean trade to include the east African coast and the opening of the trans-Saharan trade routes in the early centuries CE. Full integration of sub-Saharan Africa into the greater world of Afro-Eurasia would not occur, however, until the late first millennium CE and the expansion into the Sahel of the new civilization of Islam.

By contrast, the separation of the Americas would last for more than another millennium. Despite the separation, however, developments in the Americas paralleled in many ways those in Afro-Eurasia. Climatic deterioration and excessive human predation exterminated much of the Western Hemisphere's *megafauna* (large animals) after the end of the ice age a little over ten thousand years ago, as a result pushing Native Americans toward increasing reliance on diverse food sources and ultimately on agriculture. By 300 CE substantial kingdoms that were characterized by extensive social and religious hierarchies flourished in both North and South America; these included the Olmec and Maya in Meso-America (stretching roughly from middle Mexico to Central America) and the Moche in coastal Peru. Complex networks of trade routes connected these kingdoms, bringing them luxuries required for religious and social rituals such as jade, feathers, and cacao and spreading their influence north toward the American Southwest and east toward the Amazon basin. The resulting cultural traditions would last until the Spanish conquests of the sixteenth century CE violently and catastrophically ended their separation from Afro-Eurasia.

Separation from the civilizations of Afro-Eurasia would last longest in Oceania in the south Pacific. Settlers of this region were the ancestors of the contemporary Polynesians; these peoples moved into the island world of the Pacific Ocean probably from a home somewhere in southeast Asia, bringing with them a horticultural-based culture archaeologists call Lapita and a remarkable sailing technology based on the outrigger canoe. By late antiquity they had occupied Taiwan, the Philippines, and the rest of the offshore islands of east Asia and had begun to expand into the Pacific, reaching as far as Samoa, Fiji, and Tonga. By the time European mariners encountered them on a large scale and began to disrupt their cultures in the eighteenth and nineteenth centuries CE, their expansion had reached virtually every inhabitable island and island group in the Pacific, from New Zealand in the south to Easter Island in the west.

In a passage well known to explorers and cartographers in Renaissance Europe, the first-century CE Roman philosopher and dramatist Seneca[2] predicted that the whole world would one day become known: "There will come an age in the far-off years when Ocean shall unloose the bonds of things, when the whole broad earth shall be revealed, when Tethys[3] shall disclose new worlds and Thule[4] not be the limit of the lands." Only with the voyages of Columbus and his successors in the fifteenth and sixteenth centuries CE would Seneca's prophecy come true and globalization extend to the world as a whole. Until then the limits of the known world remained much as they were in 300 CE, and it was still possible for people throughout Afro-Eurasia to consult the *Geography* of the second-century CE Alexandrian geographer Ptolemy, where copies were available, for an authoritative summary of the current state of geographical knowledge.

CHAPTER 1

The New World of the Early First Millennium BCE

(ca. Twelfth–Eleventh Centuries BCE)

Sometime in the first half of the twelfth century BCE Egyptian artisans inscribed on the walls of the Theban mortuary temple of the Pharaoh Ramses III a vivid account of disasters that befell the kingdoms of the eastern Mediterranean basin. "The foreign countries made a conspiracy in their islands. All at once the lands were removed and scattered in the fray. No land could stand before their arms, from Hatti, Kode, Carchemish, Arzawa, and Alashiya on, being cut off at [one time]."[1]

When Ramses III ordered that this text be inscribed in his mortuary temple, he did not know it, but these events marked the beginning of a true "crisis of the old order" that ultimately would destroy the world he and his contemporaries knew. Over the next two centuries similar upheavals occurred throughout Afro-Eurasia, ending almost half a millennium during which a series of regional empires and kingdoms had fostered a precarious stability over much of the vast territory from the Atlantic to the Pacific.

Historians disagree about the nature and causes of the crisis. Numerous works written centuries later, such as Homer's *Iliad* and *Odyssey* and the great Indian epic, the *Mahabharata*, purport to recount events of the period. Separating facts concerning the late second millennium BCE from fiction in these works is, however, difficult. It is understandable, therefore, that Ramses III seized on the aspect of the crisis that was most obvious to its contemporaries to explain it: barbarian migrations. In the reliefs that accompanied his inscription, Ramses's artists depicted whole peoples on the move. Armies of warriors are shown accompanied by their families on wagons and their herds. Ramses was not alone in

The 1186 BCE attack on Egypt by the Sea Peoples is depicted in reliefs at the mortuary temple of Ramses III at Thebes. In this scene, Egyptian troops attack Sea People forces defending their families, who are accompanying them in ox-drawn carts. The stylized Anatolian features of the women suggest that the Egyptians believed some of the invaders came from what is now Turkey. H. H. Nelson, *The Earliest Historical Records of Ramses III*, vol. 1 (Chicago: University of Chicago Press, 1934), plate 34. Courtesy of the Oriental Institute of the University of Chicago

looking to migrations to explain the changes that were reshaping his world. The ancient Greeks also told stories of an age of migrations after the Trojan War, as did the authors of the *Rig Veda* in India and Chinese historians at the other end of Afro-Eurasia.

The migrations were not the cause but a symptom of the crisis. The underlying causes that simultaneously throughout Afro-Eurasia undermined kingdoms and empires and impelled peoples on their peripheries to seek new homes probably varied from region to region, but one overarching factor is attracting more and more attention: climate change.[2] Increasing evidence indicates that Afro-Eurasia entered a period of renewed global warming in the late second millennium BCE that resulted in a sharp northward movement of the southern border of the continental rain belts from the latitude of the Sahara to north of the Mediterranean. The result was continent-wide droughts that struck the civilizations of western Asia with severe famines and undermined their political systems and economies.

Simultaneously, farther east, drying weather in central Asia drove herding peoples, whose populations had grown in the more favorable conditions of the mid-second millennium BCE, to seek new pasture for their animals in the territories of the agriculturally based states that bordered the steppes. As a result, by the beginning of the first millennium BCE political conditions had changed radically throughout Afro-Eurasia. While similar developments occurred throughout the region, the changes were most dramatic in western Asia and northeast Africa.

A glance at a political map of western Asia and northeast Africa in the late second millennium BCE reveals a plethora of small and middle-sized kingdoms, city-states, and semi-nomadic herders extending from the Mediterranean deep into Iran. Although alliances between these states shifted constantly and wars were common, the region as a whole had enjoyed a precarious but nevertheless real stability and prosperity for almost three centuries thanks to the political order provided by five great kingdoms: the Hittites, Egypt, Assyria, Babylon, and Elam.

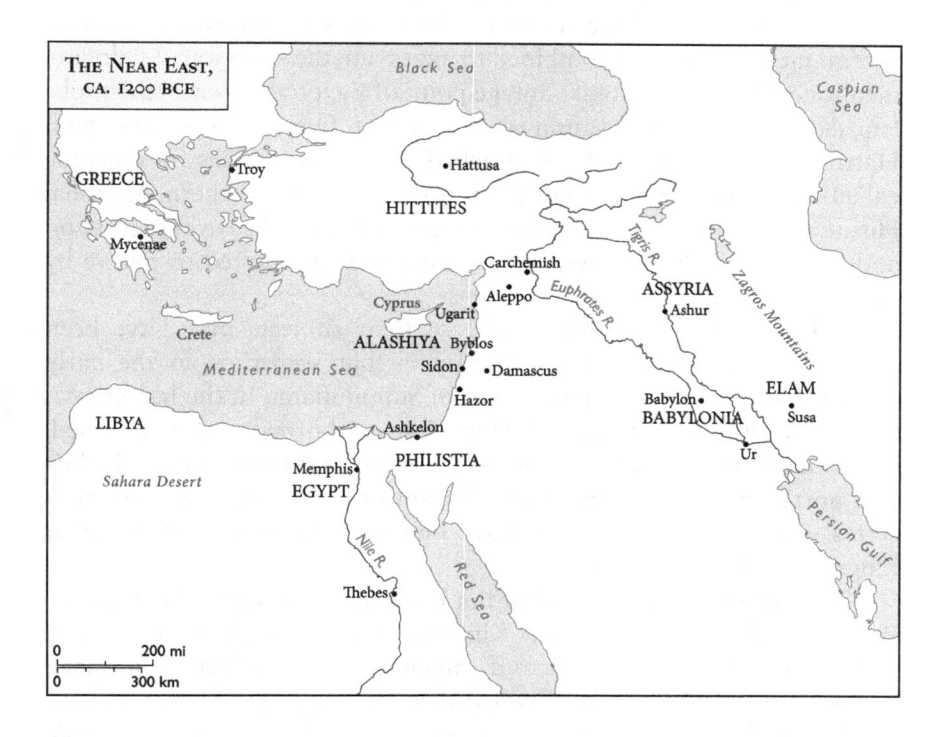

Ancient shipwrecks like that discovered at Ulu Burun in southern Turkey reveal that these kingdoms were also a part of complex trade networks that moved luxury goods such as lapis lazuli from Afghanistan, hippopotamus and elephant ivory, ostrich eggs, and ebony from Egypt and Nubia, and perfumes from the Aegean and essential metals like gold from Egypt, copper from Cyprus, and silver and tin from Anatolia. It was this vast and complex political and economic order that unraveled in the twelfth and eleventh centuries BCE.

The first signs of the crisis appeared in the early twelfth century BCE, when the two greatest states—the Hittite Empire in the north and the Egyptian Empire in the south—came under attack. Hardest hit was the Hittite Empire. Descendants of Indo-European speakers, the Hittites had entered Anatolia over a thousand years earlier. For more than two centuries they had ruled from their capital Hattusas near modern Ankara a powerful empire that covered most of present-day Turkey and Syria. Although vast, the empire was loosely organized, being composed of a variety of regional kingdoms, city-states, and tribal peoples that were held together by a complex system of vassal treaties that defined their obligations to the Hittite Great King.

The full nature of the threat to the Hittites is unknown, although several factors probably combined to aggravate the situation. As already mentioned, from the distant vantage point of Egypt, the root of the problem seemed to be barbarian invasions, and, in fact, the imperial capital Hattusas had repeatedly been attacked over the centuries by a people called the Kaskas, who lived in the mountains of northern Anatolia. Hittite sources, however, also mention conflicts over the royal succession and famine, which the government desperately attempted to relieve by importing grain from Syria.

Other factors including revolts of their subjects may have been involved. What is known for certain is that sometime in the early twelfth century BCE during the reign of Suppiluliama II, the last known Hittite Great King, the capital Hattusas was burned and abandoned. The empire collapsed, leaving in its wake throughout southern Turkey and northern Syria a disparate collection of petty kingdoms and city-states whose rulers claimed to have inherited the mantle of the great kings of the Hittite Empire.

The fate of Egypt was similar but less extreme. Like the Hittites, the Pharaohs of the Egyptian New Kingdom also had built a vast empire in the second half of the second millennium BCE, which at its peak extended from Palestine southward through Egypt for almost a thousand miles from the Mediterranean to the fourth cataract of the Nile and westward for hundreds of miles into Libya. Also like the Hittites, during these centuries Egypt experienced repeated conflicts over the royal succession, famines, and foreign invasions. Again like the Hittites, these problems reached a climax in the early twelfth century BCE, when during the reign of Ramses III Egypt suffered three major attacks by coalitions of foreign invaders: one launched from the east by migrating tribes historians call the Sea Peoples and two from the west led by the Libyans in alliance with various sea raiders.

Unlike the great kings of the Hittites, however, Ramses III succeeded in beating off the invaders. His victories did not end the crisis, but they did buy the Egyptian Empire another century of existence. Nevertheless, by the end of the New Kingdom in 1069 BCE Egypt had lost its imperial territories outside the Egyptian homeland. Ironically, the decisive blow was self-inflicted, a civil war caused by the attempt of Panehsy, the governor of Nubia, to seize control of Upper Egypt. Although Panehsy was driven back into Nubia after bitter fighting, Egypt lost its vast Nubian empire and with it access to the luxury products and gold that had made Egypt's wealth legendary in the second millennium BCE.

Still, Egypt survived, but only as a severely weakened regional power. An Egyptian ambassador named Wenamun learned how far Egypt had fallen from the glorious days of the New Kingdom three centuries earlier when he attempted to obtain cedar at Byblos for the temple of Amun at Thebes. His request was contemptuously rebuffed by the local ruler with the comment: "I am not your servant, nor am I the servant of him who sent you."[3]

Like nature, politics abhors a vacuum. The disappearance of the Egyptian and Hittite empires encouraged their eastern neighbors Assyria and Elam to dream of replacing them. Assyria was the first to move. After being only a minor regional kingdom, whose territory was limited to the city of Assur in northern Mesopotamia for much of the second millennium BCE, Assyria had succeeded in elbowing its way into the ranks of the great kingdoms over the protests of Babylon and the Hittites in the fourteenth century BCE. During the next two hundred years, ambitious Assyrian kings like Tikulti Ninurta I in the thirteenth century BCE and Tiglath Pileser I a century later built an empire that ultimately included Syria, much of southern and eastern Anatolia, and even their former suzerain Babylon. Assyria's triumph was brief, however. Invasions by Aramaean nomads from their home in eastern Syria destabilized the whole of Mesopotamia until, by the early eleventh century BCE, the Assyrian Empire had disappeared.

While Assyria was occupied in the north and west, Elam, which already had united most of southwestern Iran into a powerful kingdom, contested Assyrian dominance of southern Mesopotamia. In the mid-twelfth century BCE the Elamite king Shutruk-Nahunte claimed the throne of Babylon, and when his claim was rejected, he captured and sacked Babylon. He brought back to his capital Susa numerous historical monuments including the stele containing the *Law Code of Hammurabi*, where French archaeologists found it early in the twentieth century. However, Elam's pre-eminence proved to be as ephemeral as that of Assyria. Before the Elamites could consolidate their hold on southern Mesopotamia, they lost control of Babylon to a rebel king named Nebuchadnezzar I, who succeeded in sacking Susa and destabilizing the still fragile Elamite kingdom, which disintegrated sometime in the early eleventh century BCE.

The result of almost a century and a half of political and military upheaval was a virtually unparalleled situation. None of the great empires and major kingdoms that had provided the framework for political and economic life in western Asia was still standing at the beginning of the eleventh century BCE. The next three centuries were a period of revolutionary change, but writing its history is difficult. Written sources in the ancient Near East were produced in periods of political and military expansion, so that when the Bronze Age empires and kingdoms collapsed, our textual sources also disappeared. The same is true of archaeological evidence, since monumental building and art and the long-distance trade in luxuries and metals both contracted sharply for the same reason.

In view of the magnitude of the changes that occurred in the late Bronze Age, it is understandable that contemporaries like Ramses III, the Egyptian author of the "Report of Wenamun," and Babylonian authors of Job-like meditations on the place of evil in the world, were primarily impressed by the chaotic conditions of the new age, despairingly observing,[4] "I have looked around in the world, but things are turned around; the god does not impede the way of even a demon." From their point of view, centuries of political order, prosperity, and stable moral values had been replaced almost overnight by political disorder, radical social change, and widespread poverty.

Viewed from the perspective of their former subjects and the peoples beyond their borders, however, the situation would have looked very different. Difficult though conditions may have been, the collapse of the great powers opened a unique period of opportunity for them. This window of opportunity was brief, lasting for less than three centuries until the resurgence of Assyria in the ninth century BCE again subjected most of the ancient Near East to the rule of an imperial power. During this brief but exceptional period, however, new peoples and states formed including the Phoenicians, Hebrews, Nubians, Persians, and Greeks, who would play fundamental roles in the events of the succeeding millennium.

The most far-reaching changes were in Anatolia, where the collapse of the Hittite Empire freed its subjects to seek their place in the sun. The most successful were the Phrygians—possibly immigrants from southeastern Europe—who built a kingdom that embraced most of the former Hittite heartland in central and western Anatolia, which they ruled from their capital at Gordion, modern Yassthüyük. Elsewhere in western and southern Anatolia and northern Syria a dizzying variety of major and minor kingdoms, tribal federations, and city-states emerged from the disintegration of former Hittite provinces. At the same time, southeast of Anatolia the decline of Assyria and Babylon enabled Aramaean nomads to migrate from the Syrian homeland and found a series of petty kingdoms throughout northern Syria and Mesopotamia, while the fragmentation of the Elamite kingdom allowed various Indo-European peoples, including the Medes and Persians, who had entered Iran from central Asia, to establish themselves.

By contrast, tracing the impact of the breakup of the Egyptian Empire on the peoples of southwest Asia and northeast Africa ought to present few problems. Unlike the situation in Anatolia and Mesopotamia, the sources are relatively abundant and reflect both Egyptian and non-Egyptian perspectives on the process. Ironically, however, that is the problem, since for a large part of the history of the early first millennium BCE historians depend on one non-Egyptian source, whose reliability is controversial: the Bible.

At first glance, this is strange, since, uniquely in ancient Near Eastern history, the historical books of the Bible from Joshua to Second Kings seem to provide a detailed and circumstantial account of events in Syria-Palestine from the twelfth century BCE to the early sixth century BCE. Almost two centuries of scholarly investigation, however, have raised serious questions about the accuracy of much of this account.[5] The problems are fourfold. First, the authors of the biblical narrative relied on lost sources of uncertain character and reliability for their account of events that took place half a millennium earlier than its composition in the mid-first millennium BCE. Second, archaeological confirmation is lacking for important aspects of the biblical story such as the Hebrew conquest of Judaea and the great empire of David and Solomon. Third, much of the detail of the narrative, such as the numerous speeches and dialogues, are clearly fictitious. Fourth, the interpretation of events in the biblical account is seriously anachronistic, reflecting religious ideas of the mid-first millennium BCE and not its beginning.

Historians, as a result, have learned to exercise care in using the biblical account of events in the early Iron Age and accept that some of the best known stories of the Bible, including many of the details of the Hebrew conquest of Judaea and the reigns of David and Solomon, may not be historical. Nevertheless, when the biblical narratives are interpreted in the light of Egyptian and Assyrian texts and archaeological evidence, a relatively clear picture emerges of conditions in Syria-Palestine at the beginning of the first millennium BCE. What stands out is that, except for rare incursions such as the campaign of the Pharaoh Shoshenq I in the late tenth century BCE, Egyptian influence in Syria-Palestine had completely disappeared, thereby liberating Egypt's former Canaanite subjects.

During the New Kingdom, Egypt's empire in Canaan had consisted of a series of city-states and petty kingdoms ruled by client kings and reinforced by forts and garrisons established at strategic points. With the collapse of the Egyptian Empire, all these states regained their independence. Of all Egypt's former Asian subjects, however, it was the port cities occupying the coast between Tyre in the south and Aradus in the north—the region the Greeks later called Phoenicia— that emerged from the late Bronze Age crisis with the least damage and continued Canaanite traditions into the first millennium BCE.

The experience of the five cities located farther south in present-day Israel from Ashdod to Gaza was less happy. Archaeological evidence reveals a radical change in their material culture at the beginning of the first millennium BCE, at the same time that the Bible depicts them as ruled not by Canaanites, but by a new people, the Philistines. Their identity is unclear, but historians usually identify the Philistines with the Peleset, one of the diverse groups of raiders Egyptians called the "Sea Peoples," and view them as immigrants from the Aegean because of the close relationship between various aspects of the material culture of the Philistine cities and late Mycenaean culture, particularly their architecture and abundant painted pottery.

Meanwhile in the interior of what is now Israel and Jordan, new states formed under the pressure of the Philistine cities trying to extend their influence into the interior to protect the Arabian and Mesopotamian trade routes on which their prosperity depended. By the tenth century BCE the two kingdoms of Israel and Judah had taken shape around the cities of Samaria and Jerusalem in the hill country of Israel while across the Jordan River the kingdom of Moab had come into existence. More complicated, however, was the impact on Egypt itself and its neighbors in northeast Africa.

Egypt emerged from the collapse of its empire impoverished, divided, and under foreign rule for the first time in over half a millennium. The pharaohs of the late New Kingdom had encouraged the settlement of Libyans in Egypt and the recruitment of Libyans into the Egyptian army. The growth in their numbers, however, tipped the balance of power in Egypt against the native Egyptian population. By the tenth century BCE Libyans dominated the Egyptian army and occupied the highest positions in the government. Finally, a Libyan chieftain named Shoshenq seized the throne in 945 BCE, founding the twenty-second dynasty and opening a period of more than two hundred years of Libyan rule in Egypt.

Although Libyan chieftains were recognized as pharaohs in Egypt, they resisted full integration into Egyptian society, as evidenced by their retention of their non-Egyptian names and tribal titles, preference for submitting decisions to oracles for approval, and, most important, practice of filling government office by grants to fellow kinsmen, which quickly became hereditary. Declining royal power and increasing political fragmentation were the inevitable results, until by the late eighth century BCE Egypt was divided into at least ten separate political units, four of which were ruled by Libyan chiefs who each claimed to be pharaoh.

As in Syria-Palestine, a divided and weakened Egypt also created opportunities for its former subjects in Nubia. Egypt had governed its Nubian empire during the New Kingdom by relying on local leaders in the central Sudan, who had been co-opted into the system. The end of Egyptian rule freed them to pursue their own goals, and although the details are lost, American excavation of the royal cemetery at el-Kurru near the fourth cataract of the Nile has documented the gradual transformation of a series of regional chieftains into kings ruling the entire upper Nile Valley in Egyptian style. The process began in the early ninth century BCE with burials in Nubian-style tumulus—large mounds—tombs and ended in the late eighth century BCE with Egyptian-style burials in pyramids.

The Nubian kingdom was vast and complex, extending from the first cataract of the Nile in the north to somewhere south of the fifth cataract. Most of its population were farmers, who lived in villages by the Nile; inhabiting the eastern desert between the river and the Red Sea were tribes of pastoralists who migrated with their herds and who recognized the authority of the kings of Kush. Underpinning the kingdom's economy was agricultural produce supplemented by various products from the African interior including ivory, ebony, animals and their hides, and slaves, together with gold from the eastern desert.

Administration focused on a series of towns built around Egyptian-style temples between the third and fifth cataracts of the Nile of which the most important was Napata, traditionally believed to be the southern home of the Theban sky god Amun and the site of the king's coronation. At the top of the system was the king; he was chosen from a group of potential heirs whose mothers belonged to a privileged class of court women holding the title of king's sister, and he was believed to rule as the choice of Amun.

The ramifications of the crisis did not stop at the western Asian and north African shores of the Mediterranean but extended westward into the southern Balkan peninsula. Here an Indo-European warrior elite, who spoke an early form of Greek, had established a number of small, bureaucratically administered kingdoms centered on hilltop fortresses; these were home to an elegant culture influenced by the civilization of Minoan Crete that historians call Mycenean civilization. From the fifteenth to the late thirteenth centuries BCE Mycenaean warriors, artisans, and traders were common sights from Anatolia and Syria-Palestine in the east and Egypt in the south to Sicily and south Italy in the west, and then disaster struck.

Our only contemporary sources are the clay tablets that contain administrative records written in an early form of Greek in a syllabic script called Linear B. They give no hint of impending crisis right up to the moment of the fortresses' destruction, but the results are clear. Between 1200 and 1100 BCE all the fortresses were burned and abandoned and with them disappeared all trace of the civilization to which they were home including the knowledge of writing, fresco painting, and luxury metal-working. Some Mycenaean Greeks may have escaped and joined the Sea People raiders while others settled in Cyprus and the coastal cities of southern Palestine, if the Philistines have been correctly identified as Aegean refugees. At home, however, all trace of Mycenaean civilization had disappeared by the beginning of the first millennium BCE. Barely a third of the population that had lived in Greece two centuries earlier survived, living in tiny villages with only myths and legends to explain the ruins of past greatness that surrounded them.

Contact between the civilizations of western Asia and the peoples of the central and western Mediterranean and continental Europe had always been limited, so there are few traces of the Mycenaean crisis north and west of Greece. Instead, the late second millennium BCE and the early first millennium BCE were centuries of remarkable growth. The same climatic changes that brought famine and economic decline to Egypt and western Asia fueled agricultural expansion and population growth in central and western Europe. Bronze metallurgy increased in scale and quality, producing a wide variety of tools, vessels, and especially weapons for a new warrior elite that ruled the rapidly growing number of agricultural villages from hilltop fortresses that appeared for the first time throughout the region.

While the evidence for conditions south of the Mediterranean in Africa is much more limited, the little that there is points to a similar emergence of warrior elites, probably Berber speaking; they exploited the diffusion of the horse and chariot from Egypt to establish control over the agricultural and pastoral populations that inhabited western North Africa and the central Sahara. Farther west in southern Mauretania, however, the climatic changes of the late second millennium BCE led to moister conditions, which encouraged the appearance of the Titchitt Tradition, the first proto-urban culture based on mixed agriculture and associated with villages built extensively of dry stone in sub-Saharan Africa.

Far-reaching changes also occurred in south and east Asia at the end of the second millennium BCE. The nature of the evidence for these developments varies, however, in accordance with the cultures of the regions. In India, reflecting the priestly origin of most writers and scholars, the principal written sources available to historians are the large body of hymns to the gods and ritual texts known as the *Vedas*, which are difficult to date and contain few explicit references to contemporary events. Archaeological evidence is limited because of the use of perishable materials for building in south Asia. By contrast, historical sources for events in east Asia are relatively abundant, although they mostly date from the late first millennium BCE. Thanks to the central importance of an ancestor cult in Chinese culture, however, an abundance of funerary remains survive, and archaeology is just beginning to tap these riches. As a result, the outlines of the major developments are relatively clear.

Unlike the situation in western Asia and northeast Africa, the changed conditions of the early first millennium BCE in south Asia were not the result of a brief crisis, but the culmination of developments that had begun half a millennium earlier with the collapse of the Indus Valley civilization. Historians once explained these events as the result of the

Aryan invasions, the eruption into India of hordes of Indo-European-speaking cattle herders led by fierce chariot warriors from central Asia; they were thought to have destroyed the Indus Valley civilization and its rigidly planned cities, and conquered the dark-skinned survivors, whom they either subdued or drove into the southern part of the subcontinent. Archaeological and linguistic evidence suggest, however, a less dramatic explanation of the Indo-European presence in south Asia.

Excavation of Indus Valley sites has revealed no evidence of violent conquest, suggesting that the Indus Valley civilization had already collapsed when the Indo-Europeans entered India. In addition, the close linguistic relationship between the Sanskrit of the *Vedas* and Avestan, the earliest known Iranian language, suggests that the Indo-Europeans did not enter India all at once but gradually over a period of centuries, with some groups remaining in central Asia near early Iranian populations until late in the second millennium BCE. Finally, references in the *Vedas* and in the oral traditions that lay behind the *Mahabharata* point to conflicts between various Indo-European groups as well as with native Indian populations.

Instead of a sudden and violent invasion that destroyed the Indus Valley civilization, small groups of Indo-Europeans, pushed by worsening climatic conditions in central Asia, probably took advantage of the vacuum created by the collapse of the Indus Valley civilization to infiltrate gradually into northwest India in search of new pasture for their herds, founding new societies in the process. According to the hymns preserved in the *Rig Veda*, these societies were organized according to the Varna system, which was established at the beginning of time. The four classes of humanity were brought into being: Brahmins or ritual specialists, Kshatriyas or warriors, Vaishyas or herders and merchants, and the Shudras or servants, who were required to serve the first three Varnas. The gods created them from the parts of the sacrificed body of the giant Puruṣa: "His mouth became the Brahmin; his arms were made into the Warrior, his thighs the People, and from his feet the Servants were born."[6]

The process of Indo-European settlement in India extended over centuries and led to the creation of numerous chiefdoms ruled by Kshatriya warrior elites in alliance with Brahmin ritualists, whose expertise was required for the sacrifices that were the public face of Kshatriya rule. By the beginning of the first millennium BCE the expansion of the Indo-Europeans had carried them eastward from the Punjab across northern India to the Ganges Valley. References in the *Vedas* and the epics to conflicts between Indo-European chiefdoms as well as with native groups indicate that their advance was not free of conflict.

The result, however, was not the establishment of societies marked by a sharp division between Indo-European rulers and native subjects assumed by the Aryan invasion thesis. Instead, as the non-Indo-European character of the Sanskrit vocabulary for agriculture and many crafts indicates, an amalgamation of the two peoples took place; in this merging the Indo-Europeans gradually transformed themselves from predominantly cattle herders into agriculturalists, thereby laying the foundation for the emergence of the first state-level societies in India since the disappearance of the Indus Valley civilization over five hundred years earlier.

Even more than the history of south Asia, the history of east Asia in the late Bronze Age is a work in progress, with every archaeological discovery having the potential of altering fundamental aspects of our understanding of that history. Ancient Chinese historians claimed that two dynasties, the Xia and the Shang—of which the greater was the Shang—ruled north China in the second millennium BCE. Before the recognition early in the twentieth century of the significance of inscribed tortoise shells being sold as amulets in Chinese pharmacies and the discovery in 1928 of the spectacular site of Anyang, the last Shang capital, with its huge palaces and temples and royal tombs, historians treated the Shang Dynasty as mythical. These discoveries brought the Shang into history.

The oracle bones were records of consultations of the gods by the Shang kings. Divination using them involved applying heat to a tortoise shell or cattle scapula and reading the answer to a question in the pattern of resulting cracks. An example is an oracle bone dealing with the birth of a child to a royal woman name Lady Hao:

> Crackmaking on *jiashen* (day twenty-one), Que divined:
> "Lady Hao will give birth and it may not be good."
> After thirty-one days, on *jiayin* (day fifty-one), she gave birth. It really was not good. It was a girl.[7]

The tens of thousands of such oracle bones that have been discovered reveal that much of later Chinese culture including the writing system and, as the oracle for Lady Hao indicates, the preference for male children was already fully developed in the second millennium BCE. The oracle bones also illuminate the nature and history of the Shang state.

Although later Chinese tradition viewed the Shang Dynasty as the rulers of north China, the oracle bones reveal a more complex situation; they show that while the Shang ruled directly a relatively small territory in the Yellow River watershed, their kingdom was the center of a

Oracle bones like this inscribed tortoise shell are primary sources for the history of Shang China. A diviner would inquire on behalf of the Shang king by applying a hot rod to a pit made in the shell and then interpret the cracks caused by the heat. The question and its answer were then inscribed on the shell, which was preserved in the government archives. Shutterstock 14969257

loosely organized network of more than thirty states that were ruled by aristocratic warrior chieftains connected to the Shang rulers by alleged ties of kinship. These sub-kings affirmed their submission to their Shang overlords by paying tribute including tortoise shells and cattle bones for divination and prisoners of war for the human sacrifices that were believed necessary to provide dead Shang kings with labor after death. The main source of such prisoners were peoples living outside the Shang tributary network.

Especially important were nomadic peoples, pushed toward the Yellow River Valley by worsening conditions in central Asia; they introduced the horse and chariot to the Shang around 1200 BCE and their remarkable Caucasoid mummies have been discovered northwest of the Chinese frontier in the Tarim basin. The oracle bones also show, however, that beginning in the early thirteenth century BCE the Shang state entered a period of decline with its home territory and the number of its tributaries shrinking; one of those breakaway tributary states, the Western Zhou, decisively defeated the Shang in 1045 BCE and replaced it as the paramount power in north China.

By about 1000 BCE the upheavals of the late Bronze Age were over. Climatic conditions had begun to improve, and the population had begun to grow again throughout Afro-Eurasia. New states had formed and innovations in political organization, social and economic life, and technology had taken place that would remain fundamental for the rest of the period covered by this book. The process, however, was not peaceful. References to conflict abound in the literature of the early first millennium BCE. Nevertheless, later generations recognized the significance of these developments and looked back on this period as a time in which models of ideal behavior and values were to be found.

CHAPTER 2

The Early Iron Age

(ca. Tenth–Seventh Centuries BCE)

In his *Works and Days*, the moralizing poem that he composed sometime in the eighth century BCE, the Greek poet Hesiod advised his ne'er-do-well brother that he should "pass by the smithy's seat and the warm talk-hall in wintertime, when the cold keeps men from their works."[1] Hesiod's casual allusion to the potential risks of wasting time at "the smithy's seat" reflects a fundamental change in the social and economic life of the peoples of western Asia and the Mediterranean basin in the early first millennium BCE. Unlike the situation in the second millennium BCE, when bronze, the principal metal, was rare and expensive, and its supply and distribution was tightly controlled by governments, the presence of "smithies," that is, ironworkers, in rural Greek villages and the growth in the number of iron objects found in archaeological sites throughout the region are clear evidence of the "democratization" of metal usage after the beginning of the first millennium BCE.

The iron revolution was the unintended result of the crisis described in the previous chapter. Iron ores are common throughout the world, and it was known already in the second millennium BCE that they could be turned into a potentially useful metal. An iron-bladed knife was found in the Egyptian king Tutankhamun's tomb, and subjects of the Hittites had learned the secret of smelting and working iron. The process was difficult, however, and the resulting metal was inferior for many purposes to the familiar bronze. But bronze had a fatal flaw. As the Ulu Burun wreck revealed, a wide-ranging trade network was required to bring together the two components of bronze: copper and tin. Copper sources were not rare; Cyprus—the copper island—was only the most important source of many, but tin sources were few, being scattered from Anatolia to the western Mediterranean and even beyond to Britain. Not surprisingly, bronze became increasingly hard to obtain as the upheavals at the end of the second millennium BCE sharply reduced maritime trade and, therefore, access to copper and, especially, tin sources. As a result, the peoples of the eastern Mediterranean basin and western Asia were forced to substitute the hitherto despised iron for bronze where they could.

Bronze, of course, did not disappear. Quite the contrary, it remained the preferred metal for weapons, armor, and all sorts of luxury metal wares where utility combined with fine craftsmanship and beauty was desired. Iron, however, particularly after smiths learned that adding carbon during the smelting process produced a hard and strong metal that could hold an edge, became the metal of choice for tools and utilitarian goods of all kinds from nails to ploughs. In a short time, metal usage ceased to be the privilege of the elite, as shown by the huge number of small iron dedications in early Iron Age Greek sanctuaries.

Inexpensive iron tools also made it possible for farmers to bring new land under cultivation and expand production, fueling population growth throughout the eastern Mediterranean and western Asia, just as the rain belts moved south again and climatic conditions gradually improved in the ninth century BCE. Not all the results of the spread of iron usage were positive, of course. The ever-increasing demand for iron tools also speeded up deforestation throughout the region as forests were cleared to provide fuel for iron smelters and to meet the food needs of growing populations so that the philosopher Plato's description of classical Attica as resembling "the bones of an emaciated man"[2] would be true of many areas of the region.

None of the cities and kingdoms of the eastern Mediterranean was self-sufficient, however, so that trade had never completely ceased despite the dangers so graphically described—piracy, robbery, extortion—in the account of Wenamun's ill-fated trip to the Levant to purchase cedar for the temple of Amun at Thebes. Understandably, the peoples of the eastern Mediterranean were suspicious of strangers in the wake of the collapse of the Bronze Age empires. On exposed islands, coastal settlements were abandoned in favor of more easily defended interior sites, and the limited sea-borne trade that still existed was confined to necessities. What changed this calculus was the steadily expanding need for metals, both bronze and iron, that finally spurred a revival of maritime trade.

It was the Neo-Hittite kingdoms of Syria and the Phoenician cities of the Levant that first took advantage of the new trade opportunities. Neo-Hittite-style lions in archaic Greek art and dedications in Greek sanctuaries of spectacular tripods and cauldrons decorated with griffin heads that were ultimately based on central Asian models reveal the existence of trade routes that ran from central Asia through Anatolia and Syria to the Mediterranean. The lion's share of the new trade, however, was maritime, and that was garnered by the Phoenician city-states.

Much is mysterious about the Phoenicians. No Phoenician literature survives, so they are known only from what the peoples they encountered said about them; and much of that is hostile, highlighting strange customs such as the *molk*, the custom that is best attested at Carthage of sacrificing children during crises to Baal Hammon and his consort Tanit. Even their name—Phoenician, the "Purple People"—is foreign, given to them by the Greeks, who associated them with the rich textiles colored with the purple dye they made from a mollusk known as the murex, huge numbers of whose shells are found at Phoenician sites throughout the Mediterranean.

What is clear is that with the possibility of expansion into the interior of western Asia cut off by the coastal mountains of the Levant, the Phoenicians looked westward across the Mediterranean for commercial opportunities, and they quickly became familiar figures throughout the eastern Mediterranean. Homer knew them as wily traders from the city of Sidon, who brought the Greeks spectacular textiles, metal wares, and jewelry, but who were also treacherous slavers. The Bible's picture is more positive. According to the author of the First Book of Kings,[3] the king of Tyre partnered with Solomon in the building of the first temple in Jerusalem and helped the Judean king build ships for commercial expeditions in the Red Sea. The fullest picture of Phoenician trade at its peak, however, is provided by the sixth-century BCE prophet Ezekiel, who vividly evokes the wealth Tyre reaped from a trade network that extended from Anatolia in the north to Egypt in the south and westward as far as the Atlantic coast of southern Spain: "When your wares were unloaded off the seas you met the needs of many nations; with your vast resources and your imports you enriched the kings of the earth."[4]

The trade network described by Ezekiel took centuries to develop. From their first settlements in Cyprus in the ninth century BCE to Malta, western Sicily, and Sardinia, the Phoenicians moved steadily westward toward Spain in the early Iron Age. The center of the most intense Phoenician activity in the west, however, was north Africa. For almost two centuries from their foundation in the early eighth century BCE, the first Phoenician settlements in the region—Utica and Carthage in Tunisia, Gades (modern Cadiz) in the southwest of the Iberian peninsula, and Lixus on the Atlantic coast of Morocco—functioned primarily as links in the sea route that connected their mother city, Tyre, with the

The main evidence for the molk, *the Punic custom of sacrificing children during crises to Baal Hammon and his consort Tanit, is the tophets, or children's cemeteries, at Carthage and other settlements in the western Mediterranean. This stele from the tophet at Carthage shows a priest carrying a child intended for the sacrifice.* Erich Lessing/Art Resource, NY ART26582

metal trade of the far western Mediterranean and the Atlantic coasts of Europe with its rich sources of tin and especially silver.

To anticipate later events, Carthage replaced its mother city Tyre following the latter's capture by the Babylonians in 573 BCE as suzerain of the Phoenician settlements in north Africa and the western Mediterranean. By the fifth century BCE Carthaginian influence extended from Tunisia to the Atlantic in north Africa and across the Mediterranean to western Sicily and Sardinia. At home, Carthage ceased paying tribute to its Libyan neighbors and expanded its territory south and west, rapidly creating an empire that included all the Phoenician settlements as far as the Atlantic.

The creation of the Carthaginian Empire spread Phoenician language, culture, and institutions throughout north Africa and transformed the social and cultural life of the region's Libyan populations. The results were most obvious in the cities of the Carthaginian Empire. These cities were ruled by a mixed elite of Phoenicians and acculturated Libyans called Libyphoenicians by Greek and Roman writers. The military needs of the Carthaginian Empire also facilitated the emergence of the first Libyan kingdoms in north Africa. Lacking sufficient manpower to meet its military needs, Carthage relied on mercenary and allied forces recruited from tribal alliances in neighboring regions of north Africa, and the chiefly families of the dominant tribes in these alliances became the royal families of the new kingdoms. As a result, when these kingdoms finally appear in the sources in the third century BCE, we find that their governments and cultures had been strongly influenced by Carthage.

Not only in north Africa, but everywhere they went, Phoenician traders and settlers spread their version of western Asiatic culture including cults of gods such as the sun god Melqart and the fertility goddess Tanit, iron technology, bronze casting, an eclectic art that mixed Egyptian and Syrian elements, and especially their alphabet, which was easily adapted to write a multitude of languages from Spain to Anatolia. Phoenician westward expansion had its greatest impact, however, in the Aegean.

The Greek recovery from the collapse of the Mycenaean kingdoms was well under way when the Phoenicians began exploring the Aegean basin in the early eighth century BCE, probably in search of metal sources. By then, Greek settlers had reoccupied the west coast of Anatolia and founded new settlements throughout the Aeagean, on Cyprus, and on the island of Rhodes. A political revolution also was in progress throughout the region. The decentralized petty monarchies that had emerged out of the wreckage of the Mycenaean kingdoms had virtually disappeared, being replaced by the first of what would ultimately be more than a thousand *poleis*, the uniquely Greek urban form.

Although tiny, the early *poleis* already shared the distinctive feature of being fully independent city-states. With rare exceptions, each consisted of a walled central place dominating a small agricultural hinterland that was rarely more than one hundred square miles in extent. In keeping with their small size, their governments were simple, being ruled by aristocratic oligarchies supported by citizen bodies composed of the adult male members of self-sufficient agricultural households. Citizen obligations were few, primarily to defend their city and to produce by means of their wives the next generation of citizens. Citizen women were protected against outsiders by virtue of being members of *polis* households, but they never achieved active adult status, being always under the guardianship of male relatives, be it their father, husband, or even son. Beneath the privileged circle of citizens were the landless poor and an increasing number of slaves, who had to eke out a living as dependent laborers, protected only by the fickle justice of the gods.

Contact with the Phoenicians resulted in fundamental changes in the culture of the new *poleis*. Near Eastern luxuries from textiles to jewelry spread through the Aegean. Artistic themes emphasizing naturalistic forms borrowed from western Asia and Egypt replaced the geometric styles that had dominated post-Mycenaean Greek art. Phoenician artisans also took up residence in various Aegean settlements including Crete and Rhodes and introduced Greek artisans to new techniques in working metals, ivory, and other materials. The Phoenicians also were probably the intermediaries in the transmission of Near Eastern myths to the Greeks. The most revolutionary Phoenician gift to the Greeks in its impact, however, was the alphabet.

After almost half a millennium, Greeks began to write again in the eighth century BCE, but in a new way. The Phoenician alphabet expressed only consonants, not a serious problem for speakers of Semitic languages in which consonants carry the core meaning of a word and vowels secondary aspects of meaning such as tense, number, gender, and so on, which are usually clear from context. Such a system, however, couldn't work for an Indo-European language like Greek in which word roots are composed of both consonants and vowels. A single change, however, resolved the problem. A few letters of the Phoenician alphabet represented sounds not used in Greek, so adapting these letters to express vowels enabled the Greek version of the alphabet to represent any sound in the Greek language while simultaneously simplifying the process of learning to write. Thanks to these two developments, the

Greeks were freed from the scribal control of literacy that had characterized all earlier civilizations, and for the first time private individuals were able to create written texts. The personal character of alphabetic writing in Greece meant that it was even possible for elite women such as the Lesbian poetess Sappho to write poetry with a distinctive feminine point of view, such as this poem with its gentle mockery of aristocratic martial values:

> Some say a force of cavalry, some of infantry
> And some of ships is the most beautiful thing on the black earth
> But I say it is whoever a person loves.[5]

It also meant that the diversity of early Greek written texts was unusually broad, ranging from transcribed oral poetry like the Homeric and Hesiodic epics and lyric songs like those of Sappho to public documents such as laws and even ephemeral texts like graffiti, thereby laying the foundation for the emergence of Greek literature and philosophy.

Like Phoenicia, Greece was a small, poor country with little good farmland and few resources. As population grew, Greeks had to look outside the Greek homeland for new opportunities and resources, particularly metals. The result was one of the most extraordinary migrations in ancient history, a migration that began in about the middle of the eighth century BCE and continued for over two hundred years. The trigger that set off this emigration of Greeks from their Aegean homeland is disputed: land hunger, the need for metals, trade, and refuge from expanding imperial powers such as Lydia and Persia have all been suggested. What is not in doubt, however, is the result. Individual Greeks became familiar figures throughout the Mediterranean; everywhere Greeks could be found as merchants, slavers, pirates, and mercenaries. The majority of the emigrants, however, joined expeditions intended to found new *poleis*. Ultimately, when the waves of emigration finally ended about 500 BCE, the area of Greek settlement had expanded from the Aegean basin to cover a vast area that extended from eastern Spain in the west through southern France, south Italy, and eastern Sicily to the coasts of the Black Sea.

The effect of Greek emigration was extensive, but its character varied from region to region. Although Egypt and other Afro-Asiatic states were strong enough to strictly control Greek activity in their territories, its significance was great, including introducing the Greeks to the technology involved in creating large-scale stone sculpture and monumental architecture. In a few areas like Sicily and south Italy, Greeks succeeded in conquering local native populations. In places like Gaul and the

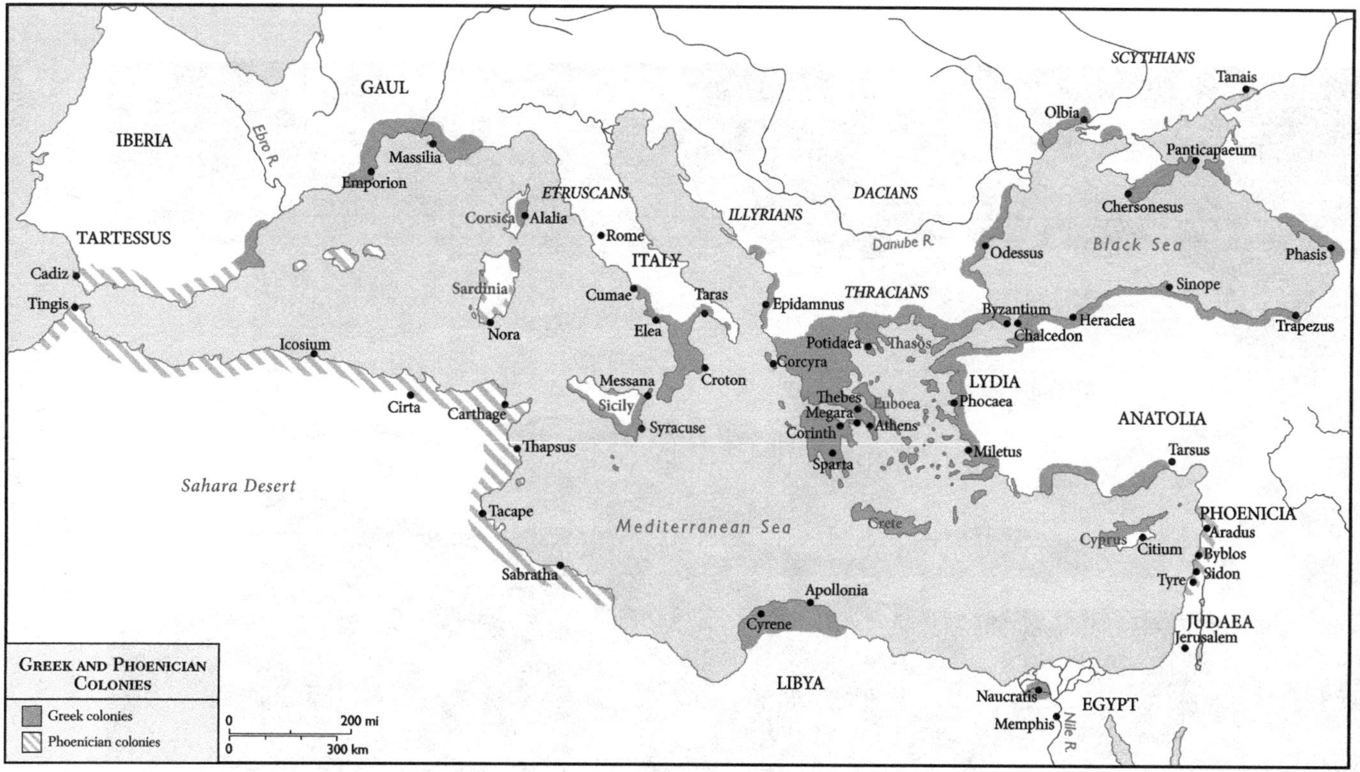

Greek and Phoenician Colonies
Greek colonies
Phoenician colonies
0 200 mi
0 300 km
GAUL
IBERIA
TARTESSUS
Ebro R.
Massilia
Emporion
Cadiz
Tingis
Icosium
Cirta
Carthage
Thapsus
Tacape
Sabratha
Sahara Desert
Corsica
Alalia
Sardinia
Nora
ETRUSCANS
Rome
ITALY
Cumae
Elea
Taras
Croton
Messana
Sicily
Syracuse
ILLYRIANS
DACIANS
Danube R.
THRACIANS
Epidamnus
Corcyra
Potidaea
Thasos
Thebes
Megara
Corinth
Athens
Euboea
Sparta
Crete
Mediterranean Sea
LYDIA
Phocaea
Miletus
ANATOLIA
Tarsus
Byzantium
Chalcedon
Heraclea
Sinope
Trapezus
Phasis
Black Sea
Odessus
Olbia
SCYTHIANS
Tanais
Panticapaeum
Chersonesus
PHOENICIA
Aradus
Byblos
Sidon
Tyre
Cyprus
Citium
JUDAEA
Jerusalem
Apollonia
Cyrene
LIBYA
Naucratis
Memphis
EGYPT
Nile R.

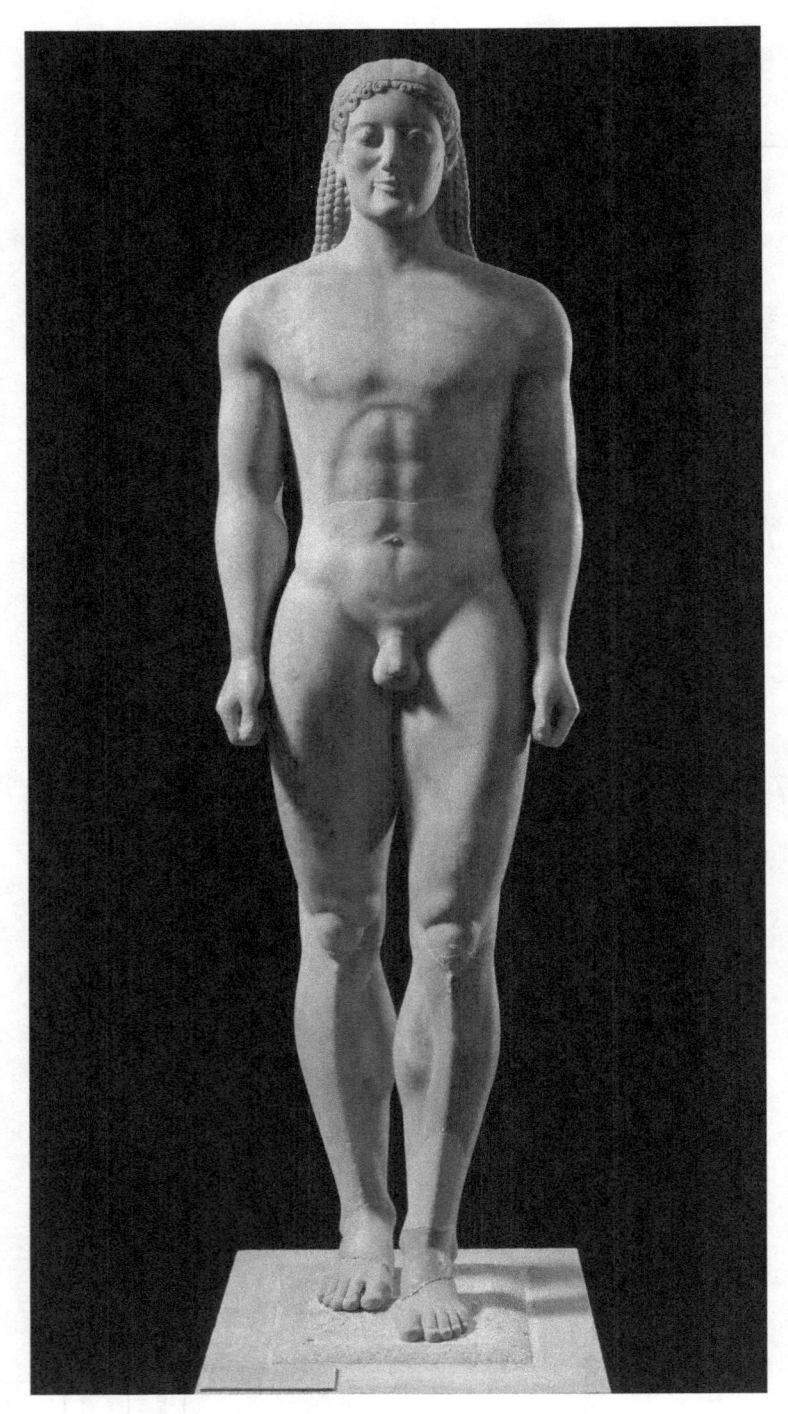

Like other archaic Greek statues, the design of the marble Anavysos Kouros *was modeled after traditional Egyptian statues—bilateral symmetry, arms held at the sides, and left leg advanced. The combination of Egyptian influence on the statue's design and the fact that its Athenian owner was named after the Lydian king Kroisos reflects the extensive political and cultural interactions in the eastern Mediterranean during the sixth century* BCE. Nimatallah/Art Resource, NY ART9089

Black Sea, however, it was the native populations that held the upper hand, and the presence of Greek luxury goods in elite native graves illustrates the diplomatic contacts that allowed the Greek settlements on their coasts to survive and their merchants and artisans to work in the interior. Most far-reaching in its impact, however, was the Greek encounter with the Etruscans in west-central Italy.

The Etruscans were speakers of a non-Indo-European language with no known relatives in Italy or the rest of Europe. By the eighth century BCE, when the Greeks began settling in Sicily and south Italy, Etruscan villages farther north in Italy were developing into city-states governed by priest-kings that were at the center of trade routes extending from Sardinia in the Mediterranean through the Alps to central Europe. It was the Etruscans' rich metal sources and advanced metalworking technology, however, that attracted Greeks to the new Etruscan cities.

The Greeks found much that was strange about the Etruscans including the high status of elite Etruscan women, who freely socialized with the male members of their families. They also feared their naval prowess, but nevertheless, Greek merchants and artisans could be found throughout Etruscan Italy. Greek-style temples and sculpture quickly appeared in the new Etruscan cities, Etruscan gods were identified with Greek gods like Apollo, Artemis, and Herakles, and the Greek alphabet was adapted to write Etruscan. Nor were these developments limited to the Etruscans, but the Etruscans in turn spread them to cities throughout central Italy such as Rome. Within a century, the pupils had caught up with their teachers as Etruscan merchants began to compete with Phoenicians and Greeks in trade throughout the Mediterranean and its European hinterlands.

The remarkable achievements of the small states located on the western periphery of Asia were made possible by the absence of great powers in the interior that could threaten them. That situation changed with the emergence of what historians call the Neo-Assyrian Empire. The first sign of danger began in the ninth century BCE, when the Assyrians under their kings Assurnasirpal II and Shalmaneser III broke out of the Assyrian homeland in northern Mesopotamia to extend Assyrian power from the borders of Babylonia in the south to southern Anatolia in the north and the Mediterranean in the west. Their gains, however, proved ephemeral. An alliance of the small states of Syria and the Levant led by the kingdom of Damascus managed to temporarily halt Assyria's westward advance, while the threat from a new power, the kingdom of Urartu located in what is now Armenia, diverted Assyrian attention

THE ASSYRIAN EMPIRE IN 671 BCE

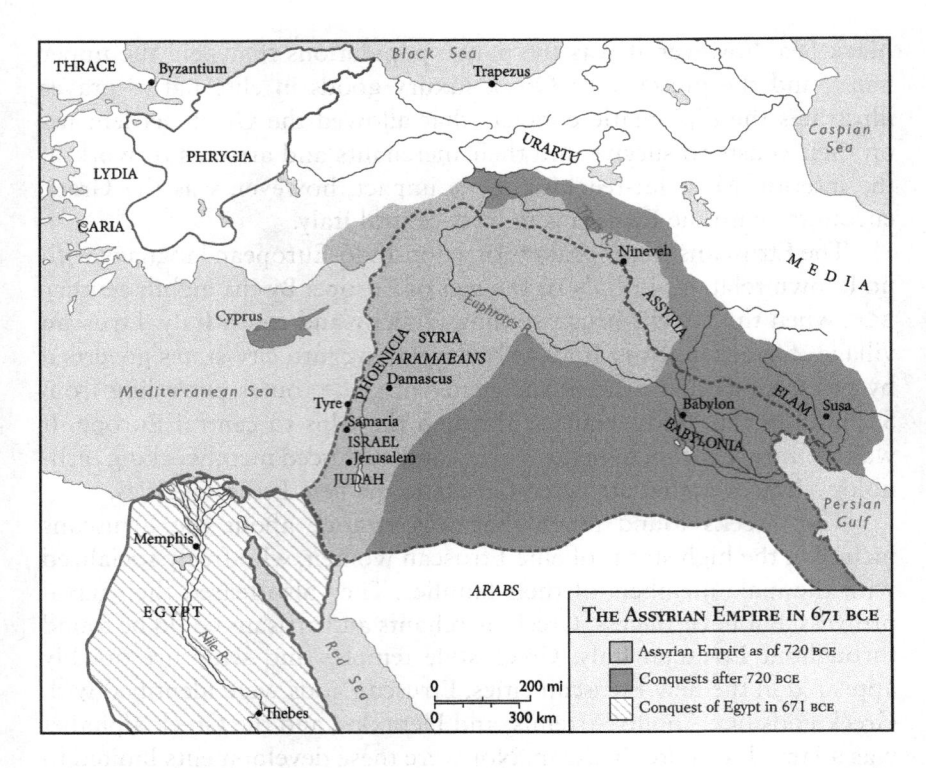

- Assyrian Empire as of 720 BCE
- Conquests after 720 BCE
- Conquest of Egypt in 671 BCE

northeastward, leaving the overextended empire unable to cope with rebellions that broke out following the death of Shalmaneser III.

A half-century later in the mid-eighth century BCE the Assyrians returned, but to a very different world. In addition to their old enemy Urartu, which had taken advantage of Assyrian weakness to extend its influence deep into northern Syria, formidable new powers had appeared. To the east, the Medes, Indo-European immigrants from central Asia, had built a loosely organized kingdom that incorporated many of the other Iranian tribes living on the Iranian plateau and threatened Assyria's eastern frontier. To the northwest in central and western Anatolia the kingdoms of Phrygia and Lydia occupied the core areas of the second millennium BCE Hittite Empire and could provide aid to potential rebels among Assyria's southern Anatolian subjects. The most formidable threat to Assyrian interest in western Asia, however, was the reappearance of Egypt as a major power.

The resurgence of Egypt was the work of the Nubian kings of the twenty-fifth dynasty. Supported by the priesthood of the god Amun at Thebes, they reunited Egypt, suppressing the Libyan chieftains, who had ruled Egypt for over two centuries, and joining Egypt and the kingdom of Kush into a single state. The result was the virtual recreation of the great empire of the New Kingdom, a kingdom that extended for over a thousand miles from near modern Khartoum in the south to the Mediterranean in the north. Within Egypt, the twenty-fifth dynasty marked a period of political and cultural revival in Egypt. Local dynasts were subordinated to royal authority and the military was strengthened. Temple construction and royal art revived. So did funerary and theological literature, all of which were characterized by emulation of archaic Egyptian styles and high-quality workmanship. Inevitably, however, the ambitions of the kings of the twenty-fifth dynasty to reassert Egyptian influence in Syria-Palestine also raised the risk of a disastrous collision with the Assyrians.

Beginning in the mid-eighth century BCE, the Assyrians reacted to the new situation with a whirlwind of military campaigns that lasted

This Sphinx with the features of the Twenty-Fifth Dynasty king Tarharqo is dated to about 680 BCE and comes from the site of Kawa in the central Sudan, the location of one of the four principal Amun temples in Nubia. The Nubian facial features of the king together with his crown indicate how Kushites adapted Egyptian art styles to express Nubian values. © The Trustees of the British Museum/Art Resource, NY ART330959

for almost a century. In rapid succession they defeated their principal enemies: Babylon, Elam, Urartu, and the Neo-Hittite kingdoms of Syria and southern Anatolia. When the peoples of southern Syria and Palestine turned to Egypt for support, the Assyrians crushed Egypt also, driving the twenty-fifth dynasty kings back into Nubia, where their successors became the rulers of the first great empire in the African interior. At the peak of their power during the reign of the king Assurbanipal in the mid-seventh century BCE the Assyrians ruled the greatest Near Eastern empire up to that time, including western Iran, all of Mesopotamia, southern Anatolia, Syria, Phoenicia, Palestine, and Egypt.

The Assyrians left a remarkably mixed reputation. On the one hand, the Persians, and after them, the Greeks, Macedonians, and Romans, viewed themselves as the legitimate successors of the Assyrians as the rulers of the *oecumene*, the civilized world known to them. On the other hand, the Assyrians were remembered for frightfulness unique in the ancient world, a reputation that they did not deny. Far from it, Assyrian royal art is replete with ghastly images of tortured and slaughtered enemies, while Assyrian royal inscriptions boast of the terror their armies inflicted. One example will suffice. The early seventh-century BCE king Esarhaddon gloated over the fate of Sanduarri, king of Kundi

The Assyrian army was the most sophisticated military force of its day. This ninth-century BCE relief from the royal palace at Nimrud illustrates its efficient siege technology, depicting a mobile armored battering ram undermining the walls of a besieged city while archers on a nearby siege tower defend it. Getty Images, De Agostini Picture Library 479640343

and Sizu, whose head he cut off. "I hung the heads of Sanduarri and of Abdimilkutte around the neck of their nobles ... and paraded (thus) through the wide main street of Nineveh with singers (playing) on harps."[6] Nonetheless, the fact remains that the Assyrians had created a new kind of empire that served as a model for all its successors.

Unlike previous Near Eastern empires, which were loosely organized conquest states primarily intended to enrich the ruling people, the Neo-Assyrian Empire was tightly structured. Outside Assyria's core area and distant subjects like the Phoenician city-states and Egypt, which were ruled by vassal kings obligated to provide tribute, conquered territory was organized into provinces administered by Assyrian governors responsible for the maintenance of order, administration of law, and collection of taxes. Moreover, for the first time in Near Eastern history, a comprehensive imperial ideology justified the creation of an empire. The Assyrian king was not only the empire's ruler. He was also priest of the storm god Assur, chief god of the ancient Assyrian capital Assur, and as such, his prime duty was to fulfill Assur's cosmic plan by extending the god's rule over the world. Just as the royal armies subdued peoples to Assur's rule, so mass hunts of lions, elephants, and other animals symbolized the conquest of nature, and, incidentally, hastened the extermination of the *megafauna* of western Asia. Resistance and rebellion, therefore, were sacrilege; and the atrocities so vividly depicted in Assyrian royal art and described in Assyrian inscriptions were the justified punishment inflicted on those who resisted Assur's will.

Fulfilling Assur's will and glorifying him with splendid temples and palaces required huge expenditures and enormous numbers of workers and soldiers, far more than the Assyrian homeland could supply. To meet the demand for labor and soldiers and also discourage rebellion, the Assyrian kings resorted to mass deportation of conquered peoples. Previous Near Eastern states had deported conquered or rebellious peoples, but Assyrian deportations were on an unprecedented scale. According to King Shalmaneser V, after the conquest of the kingdom of Israel in 720 BCE he deported 27,900 Israelites to Assyria,[7] replacing them with peoples moved from other parts of the empire.

The total number of people deported by the Assyrians is unknown— estimates run as high as 4.5 million—but the results changed the Near East socially and culturally. Whole peoples like the Neo-Hittites disappeared, losing their identity as they merged into the general populations of their new homes. The merging of populations and governments also spread Assyrian royal art and ideology throughout western Asia and the eastern Mediterranean, furnishing models for the Assyrians' Babylonian and Persian successors. So did elements of the Assyrian elite lifestyle such as eating reclining on couches, which was adopted by both Greeks and Jews, who included it in the ritual of the Passover Seder. Most important, however, the mass resettlement of Arameans throughout the empire meant the beginning of the end of Akkadian as the language of government and culture. In its place Aramaic, which was written in the Phoenician alphabet instead of the cumbersome ancient cuneiform script, became the new *lingua franca* (common language) of the Near East.

The rise of the Neo-Assyrian Empire also sparked a revival of long-distance trade to support the luxurious lifestyle of the Assyrian elite. Direct evidence for this trade is lacking, but indirect evidence in the form of the objects and materials and the terminology for foreign goods, particularly in the Bible and early Greek literature, is available and revealing. As always, the Phoenicians played a major role, providing the Assyrians with cedar wood and ivory from Syria and the Levant for building and jewelry as well as precious metals—especially silver—from the western Mediterranean. But the Phoenicians were not the only providers. Common references to various forms of incense such as frankincense and myrrh from southern Arabia—modern Yemen and Oman—attest to the opening of caravan routes from southwestern Arabia to the Mediterranean. The date of the beginning of the trade is controversial. The biblical story of Solomon and the Queen of Sheba—the kingdom of Sa'ba which controlled the southern terminus of the caravan routes—suggests a date in the tenth century BCE, but archaeology and the south Arabian alphabet, which is derived from a Syro-Palestinian alphabet related to but not identical to the Phoenician alphabet, both suggest a date in the eighth century BCE for the origin of the trade and the south Arabian kingdoms that grew rich on it.

Similarly, the reappearance of lapis lazuli in Near Eastern jewelry is clear evidence of the reopening of the trade route across Iran and central Asia to the lapis mines in Bactria—modern Afghanistan—which were its sole ancient sources. Finally, biblical and early Greek references to southeast Asian spices such as cinnamon and cassia together with their native names attest to the existence of sea routes linking the Mediterranean to south and southeast Asia. The vagueness of the information concerning the origin of many of these products in the ancient sources, however, is clear proof that few if any traders traveled the whole route between the source of many of these products and their Near Eastern and Mediterranean consumers. The fact remains, however, that for the first time since the late second millennium BCE much of Afro-Eurasia was tied together by an extensive if still fragile network of trade routes that developed to satisfy the demands of the elite of the Assyrian Empire.

In the west, intensified contact with Phoenician, Greek, and Etruscan traders had dramatic results. Large-scale silver mining in southwestern Spain near modern Cadiz spurred the development of a rich native kingdom the Greeks knew as Tartessus and Phoenicians and Jews knew as Tarshish. Similarly, small groups of rich graves full of local and imported Mediterranean luxury goods and fortified elite residences situated from the Black Sea to France on strategic points on trade routes to the European interior mark the appearance of the warrior chiefdoms characteristic of the culture archaeologists call Hallstatt. Likewise, as already mentioned, the opening of the incense trade had similarly dramatic effects in southern Arabia, where Sa'ba and other kingdoms emerged.

Farther east in south Asia, however, the situation was different. Although how spices like cinnamon reached the Near East from their sources in Indonesia is unknown, the trade itself was still in its infancy and too small, therefore, to have significant social and political effects in India. Instead, the gradual transformation of north India outlined in the previous chapter continued in the early Iron Age. Evidence of these developments is found in the ritual and liturgical texts known as the *Vedas*, the two epics—the *Mahabharata* and the *Ramayana*—and scattered references in later religious texts, and archaeology. The fact, moreover, that the fifth-century BCE grammarian Panini could refer to sixty-nine states as existing in his time suggests that extensive political fragmentation had occurred throughout north India before his time.

The new states took two forms. Kingdoms ruled by Kshatriya kings allied with Brahmin priests dominated the Ganges Valley, while in the highland periphery of the valley and the Indus Valley, states historians call "clan states" predominated. Clan states were ruled by nonhereditary Kshatriya chieftains supported by assemblies consisting of the heads of patrilineal clans composed of families drawn from the first three Varnas. Although the details are lost, three items—the legend of the war of the Pandevas told in the *Mahabharata*; a prestigious royal ritual, the horse sacrifice in which a king claimed all the territory a white horse ran through in a year before being sacrificed; and the fact that iron was adopted first in India for weapons instead of tools as in the West—allow no doubt that the process of state formation in the early Iron Age was violent.

The most important result was the consolidation of the Varna system by the definitive separation of members of the first three Varnas—Brahmins,

Kshatriyas, and Vaishyas—from the fourth servant Varna, the Shudras, by the privilege of being "twice born," that is, being initiated into the rituals of Vedism. Intensified subordination of women to their male-dominated families also is suggested by the first evidence of *Sati*, the obligation of a widow to become sanctified by being sacrificed on her husband's funeral pyre. The fact that widows could remarry, however, suggests that the sacrifice was still primarily symbolic. Finally, the corpus of the *Vedas* was completed and the foundations of Indian mathematics and astronomy were established by Brahmin scholars who had to precisely lay out sacrificial precincts and altars and determine the exact times of rituals. These changes remained central to the social and cultural life of India throughout its later history.

Even more than south Asia, east Asia remained isolated from developments in western Eurasia in the early centuries of the first millennium BCE. The Zhou Dynasty, which held a preeminent position in north China at the beginning of the millennium, was the longest-reigning dynasty in Chinese history.

According to legend, the ancestress of the Western Zhou was a woman named Jiang Yuan who became pregnant by stepping in the footprints of the Shang high god Di, thereby establishing a kinship tie between the Zhou and their illustrious predecessors. Be that as it may, for a century after the conquest of the Shang in 1045 BCE the Western Zhou expanded steadily eastward down the Yellow River to the sea, more than doubling the territory that had been ruled by the Shang. The Western Zhou government was strongly decentralized, controlling its conquests by making land grants to relatives of the royal family, who founded military colonies at strategic points in conquered territory. An eleventh-century BCE bronze vessel commemorating a victory over a Shang rebellion by the Marquis K'ang, the brother of the Zhou king, illustrates the system:

> The King, having subdued the Shang country, charged the Marquis K'ang to convert it into a border territory to be the Wei state. Since Mei Situ Yi had been associated in effecting this change, he made in honor of his late father this sacral vessel.[8]

The personal basis of the system, however, proved to be its fatal flaw, as over time the descendants of the founders of the colonies came to see themselves as hereditary rulers of their territories rather than representatives of the Western Zhou king. As a result, when the Western Zhou army was decimated in a battle in the mid-tenth century BCE, the more distant colonies began to break away and become the nuclei of independent kingdoms. The Western Zhou tried to restore control by belatedly creating a bureaucracy, but it was too late. Over the next two centuries the territories actually ruled by the Western Zhou steadily shrank and the number of independent kingdoms increased until in 771 BCE one of the new kingdoms allied with a western people derogatorily called the Quan Rong (Dog Barbarians) destroyed the Zhou capital, forcing the dynasty to flee eastward to the city of Luoyang, where their successors would reign but not rule for another five hundred years as the Eastern Zhou Dynasty.

The period of Western Zhou preeminence occupies a special place in the Chinese understanding of their past. Looking back over the violence and chaos of the Spring and Autumn and Warring States periods, later Confucian scholars and historians venerated that time as the period when familial respect and ritual governed social and political life. Although the sources allow no doubt that the reality of the Western Zhou period was far different from this idealized image, nevertheless, developments of fundamental importance for later Chinese history did take place. In government the basic model of later Chinese bureaucracies was established, while in political theory the Mandate of Heaven—the idea that extreme corruption of the ruling monarch and natural disasters indicated that Heaven had transferred the right to rule to a new and virtuous dynasty—became accepted doctrine. First used to justify the conquest of the Shang Dynasty by the Western Zhou, the notion of the Mandate of Heaven provided the basic framework for all later historical reconstructions of Chinese dynastic history. The first works of Chinese literature also were written at that time, including the earliest forms of two of the five books that would make up the canon of Confucian classics, the *I Ching* or *Book of Changes* and the *Classic of Poetry*. Finally, although China lagged behind countries to the west in developing iron technology, the thousands of exquisite cast bronze vessels, weapons, and jewelry discovered by archaeologists testify to the skills of craftsmen during the Western Zhou period.

Afro-Eurasia underwent dramatic changes during the early Iron Age. Improving climate spurred population growth from the Atlantic to the Pacific. New states and forms of states appeared that remained models for the rest of antiquity. At the same time, new technologies changed economic and cultural life. The spread of iron metallurgy democratized metal usage and strengthened the ability of people to shape the environment to their needs, a process that also would lead to massive deforestation and extermination of much of the *megafauna* throughout the region. Losses were not confined to the natural world.

While the invention of the alphabet enabled people throughout western Asia and the Mediterranean basin to become literate, it also marked the beginning of the end of the scribal cultures that had dominated intellectual life in western Asia since the fourth millennium BCE as well as the oral literatures that were the primary vehicles of cultural memory of non-literate peoples from Europe to south Asia.

CHAPTER 3

East Meets West: The Rise of Persia

(ca. Sixth–Fifth Centuries BCE)

Sometime in the 670s BCE the Assyrian king Esarhaddon asked a royal astrologer named Bel-ušezib to determine whether the stars were favorable for a campaign in Iran. Being a cautious professional, Bel-ušezib hedged his bets, informing the king that the stars indicated that the campaign would succeed, but only if the Cimmerians, "barbarians who recognize no oath sworn by god and no treaty,"[1] kept their word to not intervene. The result of Esarhaddon's campaign is unknown, but his diviner's caution was fully justified.

The inhabitants of western Asia first felt the full effect of these developments in 695 BCE, when a hitherto unknown people from the steppes, the Cimmerians, suddenly defeated the powerful Anatolian kingdom of the Phrygians and sacked their capital of Gordion. For an account of these new enemies and the threat they could pose to the agricultural states bordering the Eurasian steppe, however, we have to wait for the *Histories* of the fifth-century BCE Greek historian Herodotus, who reported that the Cimmerians' conquerors, the Scythians, "ruled Asia for twenty-eight years, and all of it was devastated because of their violence and contempt, because aside from exacting tribute from everyone, they rode around robbing whatever else people had."[2] Thus, early in the first millennium BCE a military and political revolution took place in central Asia, whose ramifications would be felt throughout Afro-Eurasia for almost three millennia.

An Iranian-speaking people, whose home was in the western Eurasian steppe, the Scythians founded the earliest known nomadic empire. The Scythians, like other nomadic peoples of the steppes, derived their power from the world's first effective light cavalry by combining two innovations: the adoption of "the good riding position," that is, seating the rider on a horse's withers instead of over its rear legs, and arming the riders with the compound bow, which enabled them to shoot arrows quickly and with great accuracy and power from a galloping horse.[3] So armed, the Scythians could cover great distances

Greek craftsmen made beautiful luxury objects for the Scythian elite. This gold vase dates from the fourth century BCE and is decorated with vignettes illustrating the life of Scythian warriors. This side of the vase depicts a warrior treating the toothache of another soldier, who carries a compound bow. Alfredo Dagli Orti/ The Art Archive at Art Resource, NY AA326195

quickly, strike with devastating force, and disappear back into the steppes.

The organization of the Scythian Empire was more complex than outside observers like Herodotus believed. They understandably focused their attention on the Scythians the Greeks encountered: the mounted warriors recruited from pastoral nomads, who lived in wagons drawn by teams of oxen during the annual movement of their flocks between summer and winter pastures. The ecology of the Eurasian steppe was more varied, however, than travelers' accounts suggested. Besides the seemingly endless grasslands of the steppes, it also included areas suited to agriculture such as river valleys and oases, so that besides pastoralists the empire also contained farming villages and urban centers. Some of these cities were huge; the site of Belsk, discovered by Soviet archaeologists in the Ukraine, had enormous walls that extended for twenty and a half miles. While farmers and city dwellers did not form part of the Scythians' fighting force, they were essential to the empire, paying it tribute and providing it with agricultural products and essential manufactured goods including the all-important compound bows, each one of which took a skilled craftsman several years of careful work to make.

The core of the Scythian Empire was a tribal alliance ruled by the leader of the principal tribe—Herodotus called them the Royal Scythians—who was supported by a personal warrior guard that accompanied him in battle while alive and joined him in death. In the end, however, the foundations of a Scythian king's power rested on four legs: membership in the royal lineage, the ability to intimidate potential rivals, winning victories, and, above all, rewarding his followers, particularly the members of his guard. The spectacular treasures of gold objects found by Russian archaeologists in the burial tumuli (artificial mounds) scattered through the Ukraine illustrate the great wealth Scythian kings lavished on themselves and their followers. Neither tribute nor loot from raiding, however, could provide the abundance of luxury goods found in the tombs, particularly the gold for which the nearest sources were either in the west in distant Europe or far to the east in the Altai Mountains. Only trade could meet the demand, and the presence of objects with Scythian animal-style decoration and other Western-style luxury goods in the remarkable frozen tombs of Pazyryk in Siberia[4] reveals that, thanks to the political needs of the Scythian kings, trade contacts extended for the first time from the western end of the Eurasian steppe to the borders of east Asia.

The irruption of the Scythians into the Near East in the mid-seventh century BCE that Herodotus described was ephemeral, but it bought the

Assyrian Empire a few extra decades of existence by distracting its enemies. While the Assyrians could still win victories over old enemies like Urartu and Elam, the reality was that the empire was overextended. The first territory to break away was the most recently acquired: Egypt. In 654 BCE, Psamtek I, the ruler of the city of Sais in the northeastern delta and the principal Assyrian vassal in Egypt, crushed the final attempt of the Kushites to regain control of Egypt. He then took advantage of Assyrian involvement in the east to rebel successfully with the aid of Aegean mercenaries provided by the king of Lydia, thereby establishing the twenty-sixth dynasty, which would rule Egypt for over a century until the Persian conquest in the 520s BCE ended native rule for more than two millennia.

Egypt was located on the far western periphery of the Assyrian Empire so that its loss, while embarrassing, was not critical. Indeed, it might even be considered advantageous since it freed the empire from the need to devote resources to defending so remote a province. Unlike Egypt, however, Babylon was critical to the empire's survival, and its loss ultimately led to the end of the empire.

The relationship between Assyria and Babylon was complex. The Assyrians venerated Babylon as the home of their civilization and expended great efforts to build libraries of Babylonian texts of all types from omen collections to epics like *Gilgamesh*. The contents of the largest such library, the one that was assembled for the Assyrian king Assurbanipal, are still some of our most important sources for the study of ancient Babylonian culture. Nevertheless, the Assyrians never found a satisfactory way to securely govern Babylon in the time they ruled Babylonia—more than a century. Alternately, they tried making the Assyrian king also king of Babylon, appointing an Assyrian governor, or establishing a Babylonian administrator.

No matter what the Assyrians did, however, the result was always the same: rebellion. Not surprisingly, in 690 BCE the Assyrian king Sennacherib took out his frustration after a rebellion in which the rebels captured his eldest son; he destroyed Babylon so thoroughly "that the site of that city and its temples would never be remembered, I devastated it with water so that it became a mere meadow."[5] As Sennacherib was murdered by two of his other sons soon afterward, it is understandable that his surviving son and successor, Esarhaddon, undertook to rebuild Babylon a decade after his father destroyed it in the belief that Marduk, Babylon's chief god, had "commissioned me for the shepherding of Assyria in order that I might appease your great divinity and assuage your anger."[6]

Esarhaddon's contrition was to no avail. Three decades later in 652 BCE, the last and greatest Babylonian revolt broke out. After four years of bitter fighting the Assyrians were victorious but exhausted, leaving them too weak to prevent Nabopolassar, the first king of the Chaldean Dynasty, from reestablishing an independent Babylon in 626 BCE. Even worse, while the Assyrians drained their remaining strength trying vainly to regain control of Babylon, the Medes, a confederation of Iranian tribes, struck, capturing and sacking the imperial capital of Nineveh in 612 BCE and putting an end to the Assyrian Empire.

The brutality of Assyrian policy had made the empire hated so it is not surprising that news of the sack of Nineveh was greeted with joy throughout the region. In Jerusalem, for example, the Jewish prophet Nahum exulted:

> Your rulers slumber, king of Assyria,
> your leaders are asleep;
> your people are scattered over the mountains,
> with no one to round them up.
> Your wounds cannot be relieved, your injury is mortal;
> all who hear of your fate clap their hands in joy.
> Who has not suffered your relentless cruelty?[7]

So completely did all memory of Assyria disappear that the Athenian historian Xenophon did not recognize the site of Nineveh when he marched by it two centuries later. Only in the nineteenth century CE did the excavations of the British archaeologist Austen Henry Layard reveal the magnificence of the ancient Assyrian capital.

The Medes had much in common with the Scythians, and like them, they had no intention of taking over the Assyrian Empire; they only wanted to loot it. The ultimate beneficiaries of their dramatic victory, therefore, turned out to be Nabopolassar and his son Nebuchadnezzar II, who took over the Assyrians' former Mesopotamian and Levantine provinces, restoring Babylon to a position of imperial power that it had last enjoyed a millennium earlier in the time of Hammurabi. Despite their achievements, however, the Chaldean kings had the bad luck that many of the sources for their history were written by their enemies. For the authors of the biblical books of Second Kings and of Daniel, Nebuchadnezzar II was not the great king of the Babylonian texts but the mad tyrant responsible for the sack of Jerusalem, the burning of Solomon's temple, and the exile of the Jewish aristocracy, while the priestly authors of the *Cyrus Cylinder* and other similar cuneiform texts ignored Nabonidus's military successes and instead luridly cataloged his alleged sins against Marduk, the chief god of Babylon, to justify their support of the Persian conquerors of Babylon.

Nevertheless, Nabopolassar and his successor Nebuchadnezzar II made the Neo-Babylonian Empire the dominant power in western Asia for almost three quarters of a century. Having secured its eastern flank with an alliance with the Medes and heavily defeated the Egyptians, who were attempting to expand their influence in Syria-Palestine, Nebuchadnezzar II consolidated Babylonian power by suppressing the few remaining independent states in the area, sacking Jerusalem and deporting the last king of Judah and the surviving members of the Jewish aristocracy to Babylonia in 587 BCE, and then gaining control of Phoenicia by capturing Tyre in 573 BCE after a thirteen-year siege. His successors extended Babylonian power into southern Anatolia in the northeast and northwestern Arabia in the southeast, thereby bringing under Babylonian control the principal trade routes linking the Mediterranean to southern Arabia and the Persian Gulf.

The importance of the Neo-Babylonian Empire was not limited to the military accomplishments of its kings. Unlike the Assyrian kings, whose inscriptions glorify the military victories they won for Assur, the inscriptions of Nebuchadnezzar II and his successors celebrate the huge palaces, temples, and walls they built at Babylon that led later Greek writers to describe it as the most spectacular city in the world known to them. Cultural developments were also significant. New versions of classic cuneiform texts such as the *Creation Epic* and *Gilgamesh* were composed, but the most dramatic advances were in science. Using mathematical techniques that later influenced both Greek and Indian astronomy, Babylonian priests were able to track the movements of heavenly bodies and even to predict eclipses with a level of accuracy never before achieved. There was more continuity in the social structure of the Neo-Babylonian Empire. The foundation of society in Mesopotamia from the beginning of its history had been the nuclear family and that remained unchanged. Male domination of Babylonian society also remained unchallenged although a handful of privileged elite women such as Adad-guppi, the mother of Nabonidus, the last king of the Chaldean Dynasty, enjoyed significant social and economic opportunities. At the bottom of the social scale, however, there is evidence for increased use of forced labor to work the estates of large landowners, and an expanded use of slaves, primarily recruited from prisoners of war and insolvent debtors, in domestic service and commerce. However, in mixed relationships, in which only one parent was a slave and the other free, the offspring were themselves free, suggesting that slavery was not yet of fundamental economic importance in Babylonian society.

More than the glory of the Neo-Babylonian Empire ended when the Persians conquered Babylon in 539 BCE after a short siege. It also marked a fundamental change in the history of western Asia as a whole: the end of the era of regional states and empires. Henceforth Babylon and its neighbors would form part of a single gigantic imperial system, the Persian Empire, that would ultimately extend from the Mediterranean to south Asia, establishing a link between these two ancient centers of civilization that would last for the rest of antiquity. Unfortunately, these important developments are among the most poorly documented in all of ancient history. Although the Persians developed a cuneiform alphabetic script to write their language, which linguists call Old Persian, they only used it for monumental inscriptions. Government records initially were kept in Elamite, and then increasingly in Aramaic, a west Semitic language closely related to Hebrew, which was written in the Phoenician alphabet. The significance of the adoption of Aramaic as the empire's principal administrative language was not limited to government, however.

Not only did the wide use of Aramaic in the Persian Empire mark the beginning of the end of the role of cuneiform in high culture that it had enjoyed since the early third millennium BCE; it also sparked the spread of alphabetic scripts from the Mediterranean to India. Ironically, however, because Aramaic was written on perishable materials like parchment or leather, few Persian documents have survived.

Still, it is clear that the Persians were an Indo-European people who had moved into southwestern Iran by the early first millennium BCE. Equally clearly, they didn't lose contact with the traditions of their central Asian home. Like the Scythians and other central Asian cavalry warriors, the Persians wore trousers instead of the robes typical of the ancient Near East and, according to Herodotus, taught their boys three things: to ride a horse, shoot a bow, and tell the truth. They also used the mysterious psychedelic drug that their close relatives, the Vedic Indians, called Soma, while the Persian king was accompanied everywhere by a ten-thousand-man royal guard, the Immortals. Also, like the central Asian nomadic empires, the principal governmental posts were monopolized by members of the royal family or of families related to it. Non-Persian officials were limited to lower level government posts or specialized court positions such as doctors.

The inadequacy of the sources also makes the rise of Persia appear more sudden and unexpected than it probably was. The sources first mention the Persians in the mid-sixth century BCE, when the Persian Cyrus II, the king of a vassal kingdom of the Medes called Anshan, revolted and overthrew his Median overlord, leaving Persia the dominant power in Iran. During the next three decades, Cyrus extended Persian power to include all of western Asia, rapidly conquering Lydia and its Greek neighbors in Anatolia, Syria-Palestine, and the Neo-Babylonian Empire. Although the Greek and biblical sources understandably emphasize Cyrus's western conquests, he also expanded Persian power eastward deep into central Asia, where he was killed in 530 BCE in the first of many confrontations between the Persians and the nomadic peoples of the steppes.

Persian expansion continued under Cyrus's son Cambyses, who conquered Egypt; and then Darius I, who seized power, founding the Achaemenid Dynasty that ruled the empire for the rest of its history. Darius also expanded Persian rule into northwest India, thereby extending the empire to its maximum extent. Darius's efforts to expand the empire westward, however, were less successful. While Macedon and Thrace fell to the Persians, his campaign across the Danube into Scythia failed, as did an attempt to gain a foothold in Greece, when the Athenians unexpectedly defeated a Persian expeditionary force in 490 BCE. Even his gains in the northern Balkans proved ephemeral, when an alliance of Greek cities led by Sparta and Athens defeated a full-scale Persian invasion of Greece in 480/79 BCE and followed up their victory by mopping up Persian outposts in the northern Balkans and liberating the Greek cities of western Anatolia and the Aegean basin.

Despite these defeats, however, the Persian Empire remained the greatest power in western Asia for almost two centuries thanks to reforms made by Darius, who reorganized and tightened its administration, dividing it into twenty provinces called satrapies and assigning fixed annual tributes to them. Each satrapy was governed by a satrap, a Persian aristocrat, appointed by the king, who was responsible for maintaining law, collecting tribute, and leading the satrapy's military forces in war.

The key to the success of these reforms was the empire's ability to rally the support of the elites of its subject peoples. Unlike the Assyrians, who tried to transform their subjects into Assyrians, the Persians did not attempt to assimilate their subjects. Instead, the Persian Empire remained, like the Scythian and other central Asian empires, a multi-ethnic entity that was united only by loyalty to the Persian king, who ruled as the representative on earth of the Zoroastrian god of light and truth Ahuramazda, and had as his principal duty defending his subjects against the supporters of Ahriman, the god of darkness and falsehood.

Nevertheless, despite the universal claims of Zoroastrianism in which all peoples were believed to be supporters of either Ahuramazda or Ahriman in a grand cosmic struggle that would conclude with the ultimate victory of truth at the end of time, the Persians pursued a policy of toleration toward the religions of their subjects, building temples and supporting their priests. The most famous example of this policy is Cyrus II's order allowing the Jewish exiles to return to Judaea from Babylon and rebuild the temple of Yahweh in Jerusalem, but similar support of local religions and the elites who led them also is documented in Babylonia, Egypt, and even Greece. For us the Persian view of their empire is still vividly illustrated in reliefs on the tombs of the Persian kings in which the king is depicted standing before a Zoroastrian fire altar on a platform held up by representations of the peoples of the empire while Ahuramazda flies above, seated on a winged sun disk. Its success is demonstrated by the loyalty of the elites of the empire, most of whom would have agreed with the Jewish prophet Isaiah, who proclaimed, after Cyrus freed the Jews from their exile in Babylonia:

The relief located above the entrance to the tomb of the Persian king Darius I at Naqsh-i Rustam in southwestern Iran. The king stands on a table held up by symbolic representations of the peoples of the empire. In front of him, the Zoroastrian god of truth and light, Ahura Mazda, soars over a fire altar. According to Persian imperial ideology, the king rules the peoples of the world as the designee of Ahura Mazda. www.BibleLandPictures.com/Alamy Stock Photo

"Thus says the Lord to Cyrus, His anointed, Whom he has taken by the right hand, subduing nations before him, and stripping kings of their strength."[8]

It is easy to underestimate the significance of the Persian defeats in the west. There is even support for such a minimalist view in the history of Herodotus, who observed that the Persians considered Persia the center of the known world and ranked peoples according to how close they were to Persia. The Persians, therefore, certainly would have considered the loss of western Anatolia on the far western frontier of the empire embarrassing but not critical so long as they retained control of the Mesopotamian and Iranian core of the empire, as they did for another century and a half, during which the Persian Empire remained the only real great power in western Asia.

Herodotus and other Greek historians didn't share this view of the Persian wars, of course. They understandably celebrated the Greek defeats of Darius I and Xerxes in 490 BCE and 480/79 BCE as glorious victories, comparable to the Greek victory in the Trojan War, the foundational event in the Greek understanding of their own history. They could point to a fact of fundamental importance in support of their view, namely, that the Greek victories of 480/79 BCE and the Persian inability to reverse those defeats in subsequent decades effectively shut off the possibility of further Persian expansion westward in the Mediterranean basin. Keeping the Persians confined to Asia, however, resulted in a revolutionary change in the nature of Greek warfare.

As befitted a people divided into hundreds of independent city-states, Greek warfare traditionally involved local conflicts and temporary alliances. Even the alliance that defeated the Persians in 480/79 BCE was little different, but to consolidate the results of the Greek victory and protect the liberated Greek cities of Asia Minor required an ongoing commitment to frustrating Persian efforts to regain their lost territories. The result was the formation under Athenian leadership of a permanent naval alliance that historians call the Delian League and that ultimately had more than four hundred members committed to supporting with taxes and manpower an ongoing defensive war against Persia that lasted until peace was made in 449 BCE. Athens could not resist the temptation to exploit its leadership position, however, so the Delian League gradually became the nucleus of an Athenian empire whose revenues funded many of the institutions of the Athenian democracy and the splendid buildings that even in their current ruined state remain the glory of Athens.

For much of the fifth century, however, the integration of much of the Aegean into a single political unit led to unprecedented prosperity

In the fifth century BCE, aristocratic Athenian boys commonly attended schools conducted by privately paid teachers. This cup by the early fifth-century BCE painter Douris depicts a boy taking literature and music lessons in such a school. Antikensammlung, Staatliche Museen, Berlin, Germany/Art Resource, NY ART177370

not only for Athens but for most of the Greek cities. That prosperity was based on trade, and a network of trade routes that extended from the Black Sea to Britain and brought huge volumes of goods as varied as grain, tin, papyrus, timber, gold, and slaves into the Aegean, but especially to Athens. In the words of the first-century BCE historian Diodorus, after the Greek victory in 480/79 BCE, "not only did the inhabitants of Greece escape from danger, but they gained great fame, and every Greek city was filled with such abundance that all were astounded at their reversal of fortune.... Greece experienced a great surge of prosperity. In this period the arts flourished because of the abundance, and the greatest artists known to posterity existed then."[9]

This impressive economic growth was facilitated by the spread of coinage, which had been invented by the Lydians in the sixth century BCE as a convenient means of storing and transferring large amounts of wealth. The addition of multiple small-denomination coins in the fifth century BCE transformed coins into the principal means of exchange for trade and permitted the monetization of large parts of the economies of the Greek cities. At Athens, prosperity brought with it fundamental changes in all areas of life. Best known are the cultural developments including the extraordinary building program for temples and other public structures, the flourishing of sculpture and other arts, and the birth of Athenian drama, philosophy, and other literary forms.

Equally remarkable was the expansion of participation in Athens's democratic government and the fleet on which the city's power depended to include citizens—male, of course—from all socioeconomic classes. While opportunity expanded for male citizens, it perversely narrowed for women. This was particularly true of women of the upper class; their ability to function freely in Athenian life outside the religious sphere was restricted by the traditional Greek view that men's space was outside the home and women's was inside. The most dramatic change, however, was the enormous expansion in the number and use of slaves in Athens; they were found in every area of Athenian economic life, including mining, crafts, domestic service, money changing, and even such governmental areas as police and administrative functions. This increased use of slave labor made Athens one of the few known slave societies in history. Even more important, the fact that the overwhelming majority of slaves at Athens were non-Greeks combined with the Greek victories over the Persians resulted in a revaluation of the concept of the "barbarian." Instead of merely designating a non-Greek, "barbarian" increasingly indicated an inferior non-Greek, whose place in society was in the view of many Greeks, including the fourth-century BCE philosopher Aristotle, that of a natural slave, a theory that was to play an important role centuries later in justifying African slavery in the Americas.

The Greeks were not the only beneficiaries of the end of Persian westward expansion. Carthage had already taken control of the network of colonies that linked Phoenicia to mineral-rich Iberia early in the sixth century BCE; then, freed of the threat of Persian conquest, it tightened its control of western Sicily and in alliance with the Etruscans, who ruled much of central and northern Italy, stopped further Greek expansion in the western Mediterranean. In Iberia, intense interaction with Carthage was reflected in the foundation of towns and the appearance of eastern Mediterranean-style sculpture. When Carthage tried to expand its colonial empire farther, pushing south along the Atlantic coast toward the west African gold fields and north along the Atlantic coast of Europe toward the tin sources of Cornwall to meet the growing demand from the economies of the eastern Mediterranean for bronze, it failed. However, the reports of the Carthaginian expedition leaders Hanno and Himilco remained fundamental sources of information concerning the geography of these areas for the rest of antiquity.

While the Carthaginians, Etruscans, and Greek cities fought to a stalemate in Sicily and Italy, dramatic changes occurred in western and central Europe. The driving force was climate change. After several centuries of warm weather that fostered widespread prosperity based on agricultural expansion and growing population, temperatures cooled sharply in the late sixth century, leading to abandonment of towns as people—particularly Celtic-speaking populations—migrated from their homes in western Europe in search of new farmlands. The insecurity of the period is evident in the new emphasis on weapons in the culture that archaeologists call La Tene and identify with the Celts. Trade between the Mediterranean and temperate Europe continued into the fifth century BCE and even expanded its scope to include Celtic mercenaries, who increasingly were found in the armies of the central and western Mediterranean peoples. The center of the trade, however, moved east from the river valleys of southern France, where Greek merchants had dominated it, to passes through the Alps, where Etruscan merchants replaced Greeks as the principal source of Mediterranean goods for the prestige economy of the Celts.

While Persian westward expansion stalled, the situation was different in central and south Asia. Cyrus II conquered Bactria, modern Afghanistan, but it was Darius I who took the momentous step of pushing south from Bactria to add the whole of the Indus Valley, essentially Pakistan, to the empire. The details are lost, but the conquest of northwestern India probably was complete by the end of the sixth century BCE. It is unknown how long Persian rule in northwestern India lasted, but Indian troops served in the Persian army that invaded Greece in 480/79 BCE, and half a century later Herodotus still included India in his list of satrapies and credited it with paying the largest tribute of any individual satrapy. Simultaneously with Persian expansion in northwest India, the political situation on the other side of the Indian subcontinent changed radically, as the kingdom of Magadha under the leadership of its two great kings Bimbisara and Ajatsatru established itself as the dominant power in the Ganges River Valley and in the process shifted the focus of Indian civilization southeastward toward its capital Pataliputra, modern Patna, and the mouth of the Ganges River and the Bay of Bengal.

The late sixth and fifth centuries BCE also saw major social and cultural changes that were fundamental to the later development of Indian civilization. Throughout the Ganges River Valley increasing trade and expanding agriculture driven by the growing use of iron tools led to the foundation of new cities. The more open society and the vibrant cultural life of those cities threatened, however, the stability of the caste system.

Teachers of doctrines ranging from materialism to atheism could be found seeking students throughout the Ganges Valley. Brahman theologians responded to these challenges to traditional Vedic doctrines by transforming the doctrine of the cycle of rebirths—*Samsara*—into a powerful justification for the traditional social order, teaching that a person's *Varna* was not arbitrary but determined by the character of his actions in a previous incarnation and that a king's primary duty was to maintain that order. Two teachers, however, whose ideas form the basis of still surviving religions, offered more far-reaching reinterpretations of Vedic thought: Mahavira, the founder of Jainism, and Gautama Buddha, "the Enlightened One."

Although much of the content of the surviving biographies of Mahavira and the Buddha is clearly legendary, there are striking similarities in the lives and teaching of both men. Both were members of elite Kshatriya families in clan states and lived and taught in the late sixth and early fifth centuries BCE. Both accepted the *Varna* system and the doctrine of *Samsara*, but they rejected key aspects of Vedic doctrine, particularly the belief in the efficacy of animal sacrifice. Both identified too great involvement with the affairs of this world as the reason people were trapped in the cycle of reincarnation. Both also taught that it was possible to escape the cycle of reincarnation by living an ethical and ascetic life with the result that their closest followers were monks who had to be supported by the charity of the mass of their followers who could not commit to the demanding monastic life. As a result, Jainism and Buddhism became, in effect, congregational churches. Mahavira's insistence on the absolute observance of the principle of *ahimsa*, "non-violence," limited the appeal of Jainism to males engaged in occupations like commerce that involved no killing of any breathing creature; the Buddha's teaching that one could overcome desire and escape the cycle of reincarnation by following the Middle Way embodied in the Four Noble Truths and the Eightfold Path was potentially open to anyone, irrespective of their *Varna*. Eventually women also could follow the Middle Way after the *Sanga* or order of monks was opened to the creation of separate orders of nuns parallel to those of monks despite the Buddha's initial resistance to such a role for them.

At first glance, these developments would seem to have little connection with the Persian conquest of the Indus Valley on the other side of the Indian subcontinent, but, ironically, it was a by-product of the

Persian conquest—the introduction of writing into India—that ultimately allowed the teachings of Mahavira and the Buddha to spread. The history of the two earliest native Indian scripts—*Kharoshti* and *Brami*—is controversial. Although they are first securely attested in the early third century BCE, it is clear that both were derived from the Aramaic script the Persians used to administer their Indian satrapy. However it happened, the introduction of writing made possible the preservation of the originally oral teachings of Mahavira and the Buddha in books that became the principal vehicles for the spread of these religions, particularly Buddhism, throughout south and southeast Asia and ultimately to central and east Asia.

Cultural exchange was not one way, however. A remarkable communication system tied the Persian Empire together. An extensive road system linked Iran to all parts of the empire, while Darius ordered both the construction of the first successful Suez canal and the exploration of the sea route from India to Persia. Darius's intent, of course, was to serve the needs of the government, and Persian inscriptions and cuneiform tablets document trips by government officials and the movement of building materials from one end of the empire to another. So, Darius boasted that

> this temple which I built at Susa, from afar its ornamentation was brought.... The silver and the ebony were brought from Egypt. The ornamentation with which the wall was adorned, that from Ionia was brought. The ivory which was wrought here, was brought from Kush and from India and from Arachosia.[10]

Inevitably, however, commercial and cultural goods also moved along the road network. Evidence is the appearance in fifth- and fourth-century BCE Greece of Indian products like peacocks and peaches, figures from Sanskrit mythology like the dog-headed people, and possibly even the idea of reincarnation, which Pythagorean philosophers taught in a form remarkably similar to that found in India. If goods and ideas from India at the far eastern end of the Persian Empire could reach the Mediterranean, it should not be surprising that literary and archaeological evidence points to widespread circulation of Persian-themed goods and ideas including metal dining ware, architectural forms, and even Zoroastrian priests known as Magi throughout the empire and beyond. In fifth-century BCE Athens, for example, the popularity of Persian-style wares and elements of fashion such as umbrellas was so great that it has been compared justifiably to the mania for Chinese styles that swept Europe in the eighteenth century CE.

While the Persian Empire tied together west and south Asia, conditions were different in east Asia. The three centuries after the fall of the Western Zhou Dynasty were a period of transition in China and in Chinese relations with the rest of Eurasia. Chinese contact with the peoples of the Eurasian steppe dated back to the Bronze Age, and the presence of Chinese silk in Celtic graves in western Europe and in Scythian tombs excavated by Soviet archaeologists at Pazyryk in Siberia is evidence of continued Chinese involvement, albeit loose and probably indirect, in trade networks that extended westward across Eurasia and northward toward Siberia as a result of the appearance of the Scythian Empire and other nomadic states. At the same time, the coincidence between Chinese expansion toward its northern frontier and the eastward expansion of steppe nomads organized in the Scythian manner laid the foundation for the confrontation between China and various groups of steppe nomads that would define the nature of Chinese relations with its northern and western neighbors for much of the rest of its history.

The most far-reaching changes, however, took place within China itself and covered all aspects of political, social, and intellectual life. Chinese tradition divided the five centuries between the fall of the Western Zhou Dynasty and the rise of the Qin Dynasty into two periods, the Spring and Autumn period and the Warring States period. One theme, however, unites them both: war. The Chinese would learn during these turbulent centuries the full meaning of the observation by Greek historian Thucydides that "war is a violent teacher."[11]

With the disappearance of the authority of the Western Zhou kings and the reduction of their Eastern Zhou successors to figureheads, the Zhou kingdom fragmented into as many as 148 separate states, some as small as a single city and others covering territories as large as a modern European state. The result was centuries of almost chronic war as larger states sought to grow by annexing smaller states. Not surprisingly, efforts were made to restrain the violence. The most important was the practice of recognizing the ruler of the strongest state by the Eastern Zhou king as protector (*Ba*) of the Zhou realm and its traditional values. So, in 657 BCE, for example, the protector at that time urged all states to avoid actions that would disrupt the traditional norms of Zhou social and economic life: "Let there be no damming of irrigation water, no withholding sales of grain, no changes of heirs apparent, no promoting of concubines to replace wives, and no involvement of women in state affairs."[12] All such efforts failed, however, with the result that by the fifth century BCE the bulk of the territory of the old Zhou kingdom was controlled by only seven major kingdoms: Yan, Qi, Wei, Zhao, Han, Qin, and Chu.

The incessant warfare of the Spring and Autumn and Warring States periods drove the process of change as states struggled to survive. Politically, the loose quasi-feudal organization of the kingdom of the Western Zhou proved unequal to the task and was replaced throughout north and central China by bureaucratically governed regional kingdoms ruled by autocratic monarchs that covered the whole region from the Yellow River to the Yangtze. Survival, moreover, required the mobilization of increasingly large armies with the result that the aristocratic chariot-based armies of the Western Zhou were replaced by infantry forces recruited from the peasantry and funded by taxes levied on agriculture, payment of which was facilitated by the invention of a uniquely Chinese form of coinage in the form of miniature tools. Technological change enhanced military power as the spread of iron technology made possible both increased agricultural output on which the system depended and also the development of new weapons such as chain mail armor and the crossbow. Socially, universal military service at the bottom of society and constantly shifting alliances at the top gradually erased the distinction between Chinese and non-Chinese peoples as non-Chinese residents of the new kingdoms were assimilated while tribes beyond their borders were pushed toward the frontier between China and central Asia. Culturally, the principal schools of thought that would dominate the intellectual life of China for the rest of its history appeared as an alternative after the traditional "learn on the job" training of the Zhou aristocracy failed to provide the new kingdoms with the trained officials they required to staff their new armies and bureaucracies.

Formal education was the solution, and "philosophers" became its providers. The earliest known philosopher was the man Western scholars know as Confucius, "Master Kong." The little that is known about Confucius's life indicates that he was born in the minor kingdom of Lu to a family belonging to the *Shi*, the lowest rank of the aristocracy, in the mid-sixth century BCE and that he believed that the solution to the chaotic problems of his time was to restore the hierarchic order of the Western Zhou kingdom through maintenance of the rituals and duties appropriate to families at every level of society from the lowliest peasant to the king. Having failed at a political career, Confucius supported himself by teaching fee-paying students how to govern by close study of the books that would become the canon of five classics. Other thinkers such as the Mohists, who denied the central importance of the family and identified material benefit as the highest good, criticized various aspects of Confucius's teaching such as his emphasis on the importance of ancestors and the elaborate funerary rituals that honored them. However, the model he created of the professional teacher, whose instruction was based on the study of a limited number of classical texts, remained standard for the education of officials throughout the later history of China and even spread to the military, where the study of handbooks of strategy such as *The Art of War* of Sun-Tzu became part of the training of officers.

To sum up: beginning in the late seventh century BCE the regional kingdoms that had dominated western Asia in the second millennium BCE and the early Iron Age disappeared, replaced by a single Persian Empire spanning the entire region from western India to the eastern Mediterranean and from central Asia to the southern border of Egypt and the shores of the Indian Ocean. Thanks to the emergence of the Persian Empire, this enormous area formed a single interconnected political and economic unit for the first time. Nor was the effect of these developments limited to the territory of the empire. The political, economic, and cultural life of peoples from the western Mediterranean to south Asia was also fundamentally changed by this development as they became connected to the network that held the empire together. While east Asia remained relatively isolated from the Persian Empire and its peripheries, it was also transformed as centuries of chronic and brutal warfare gave birth to a series of culturally homogeneous powerful kingdoms whose institutions provided the model for the later kingdoms that would rule a united China.

CHAPTER 4

The New World of the Macedonian Kingdoms

(ca. Fourth–Second Centuries BCE)

In 346 BCE, the ninety-year-old Athenian rhetorician Isocrates bitterly complained to the Macedonian king Philip II that it was "a disgrace ... to sit idly by and see Asia flourishing more than Europe and the barbarians enjoying a greater prosperity than the Greeks."[1] His bitterness was understandable. During his long life Isocrates had experienced the greatness and collapse of the Athenian Empire followed by decades of internecine warfare and social strife during the first half of the fourth century BCE as various Greek states—Sparta, Athens, and Thebes—unsuccessfully sought to recapture fifth-century BCE Athens's dominant position in the Aegean basin. Even worse, he had observed in frustration Persia's successful exploitation of Greek weakness to regain most of what it had lost as a result of its defeat by the Greek alliance at the beginning of the fifth century.

Athens's long decline began almost immediately after its greatest diplomatic success: the conclusion of a peace with Persia in 449 BCE in which the Persians finally accepted the loss of their Anatolian and Aegean Greek subjects. The immediate result was that peace freed Athens to use the allies' tribute monies as it saw fit. The next few decades were Athens's golden age. The monumental building program of temples such as the Parthenon and other public buildings, whose remains still dazzle tourists, and most of the surviving tragic and comic dramas that Greeks studied throughout antiquity and the Middle Ages were all created during these years. The Athenian historian Thucydides[2] understandably claimed that if Athens disappeared, future generations would believe that Athens's power was twice as great as it really was. Athens's prosperity, however, concealed growing tension between the Athenian Empire and Sparta and her allies.

The first sign of trouble came in 446 BCE, barely three years after the conclusion of peace with Persia, when Athens was forced to sign a thirty-year peace with Sparta after barely surviving rebellions in which she lost all her central Greek subjects. Fifteen years later in 431 BCE full-scale war—the so-called Peloponnesian War—broke out between Athens and Sparta. Thucydides claimed that he began writing his history of the war as soon as it started because he foresaw how great it would be.[3] He was prescient. By the end of the Peloponnesian War twenty-seven years later in 404 BCE, it had come to involve almost the whole world the Greeks knew. Military operations extended from western Asia in the east to Sicily in the west and the Black Sea in the north and wreaked unprecedented devastation throughout the Mediterranean.

Ironically, the magnitude of the destruction was the direct result of Athens's success in integrating the economies of the Aegean and the western Asian civilizations. Prosperity was how most Athenians experienced that integration. In the words of an anonymous Athenian pamphleteer, "it is to this same lordship of the sea that the Athenians owe the discovery . . . of many of the luxuries of life through intercourse with other countries."[4] That same integration, however, had two other more sinister consequences. First, the resources it provided enabled Athens to sustain a twenty-seven-year war and magnified the final cost, when it finally ended in 404 BCE. Second, the intense interaction between peoples from central Asia and the western Mediterranean meant that Eurasian pandemics became possible for the first time. Thucydides vividly described the horror of the first of what would become a recurrent feature of world history, the plague of 430 BCE—most likely smallpox or typhoid fever—that spread throughout the Persian Empire and Greece and cost Athens at least a third of its active duty military forces and untold numbers of women and children. Almost as bad as the disease itself was the demoralization it brought in its wake as "people dared to indulge more openly in their secret pleasures when they saw the swift change from well-being to sudden death, and from not having anything to immediately inheriting the property of the dead."[5]

The extent of the devastation was unprecedented. Athens understandably suffered the most, emerging from the war stripped of her empire, her citizen body reduced by half, and her democracy temporarily replaced by a brutal oligarchy imposed by Sparta. The effects rippled throughout Athenian society. Loss of the empire and its tribute and the escape of thousands of slaves impoverished wide swathes of the population. Farms had been destroyed throughout Attica, crippling the agricultural foundation of the city's economy. Perhaps most demoralizing of all, the enormous war casualties—five thousand dead in the last battle of the war alone, between 5 and 10 percent of Athens's adult male citizen population—left a generation of Athenian women with little hope of finding a husband and needing to support themselves in an impoverished society with no roles for independent women other than peddling and prostitution.

Destruction was not limited to Athens but extended throughout the Aegean. Fourth-century BCE Greek literature is full of accounts of cities torn apart by bitter social strife and the seizure of power by tyrants—military dictators—whose rule was tolerated because they restored a semblance of order and security. Not even Sparta, the victor in the Peloponnesian War, escaped unscathed. Its attempt to take over Athens's role as imperial hegemon in the Aegean strained Sparta's unique military-focused society to the point that a single defeat in 371 BCE set the city on the path of irreversible decline, stripping it of the bulk of its agricultural land and the community slaves—Helots—who worked it and supported the military aristocracy that constituted Sparta's citizen body. Even worse from the point of view of ideologues like Isocrates, while the Greek cities suffered, Persia prospered, successfully weathering multiple revolts and even reconquering Egypt in the late 340s BCE, almost sixty years after Egypt had successfully revolted at the end of the fifth century BCE. Most frustrating of all, however, was that the Greek cities repeatedly sought the intervention of the Persian great king to resolve their disputes, in effect, conceding to Persia the influence in Greek affairs that their ancestors had fought so hard to avoid over a century earlier.

Not surprisingly, the search for a solution to the crisis obsessed fourth-century BCE Greek politicians and intellectuals. Their efforts paralleled remarkably contemporary developments in Warring States China. Greek diplomats, for example, repeatedly negotiated common peace treaties only to have them fail and the cycle of endless war resume, while intellectuals offered themselves as teachers of and advisors to political leaders. So Isocrates repeatedly approached powerful rulers and urged them to lead a united Greece against the Persian Empire in order to enrich the Greeks by appropriating the wealth of the "barbarians" and transforming them into slaves. Other thinkers like the Athenian soldier and historian Xenophon ironically saw in Cyrus II—the founder of the Persian Empire—the model for the sort of strong leader who could save the Greeks from the disorder that was destroying them. It was the philosophers, however, who offered the most profound and far-reaching responses to the crisis.

The first Greek philosophers appeared in the Ionian city of Miletus on the west coast of Anatolia in the early sixth century BCE. Early philosophers like Thales filled the role played by priestly intellectuals in other east Mediterranean and west Asian civilizations by providing rational interpretations of traditional myths. Their innovation was that they attempted to explain the world revealed by our senses as the result of orderly natural processes without invoking the arbitrary actions of the gods.

Theories about the nature of ultimate reality proliferated during the sixth and fifth centuries BCE. Philosophers, however, devoted relatively little attention to society and its problems until the Peloponnesian War, although the sophists, professional teachers of rhetoric and other practical skills, incorporated their rationalistic approach to knowledge into their own teaching. As the upheavals in Greek society caused by the Peloponnesian War and its aftermath grew worse, however, philosophers increasingly turned their attention to the question of the nature of the just society and how to establish it.

The first philosopher we know who considered these questions was the late fifth-century BCE Athenian philosopher Socrates. He attracted students from the Athenian elite with his critical view of democratic leaders as false politicians, whose disastrous actions were based on opinion instead of truth. For the full realization of the new trend, however, we have to look to Plato, the student of Socrates who founded the Academy, the first philosophical school, in Athens in the early fourth century BCE. Plato was a charismatic teacher, whose theory that political action should be based on knowledge of the true nature of ultimate reality attracted students from all over the Greek world. Plato even attempted to implement his ideas in the Sicilian city of Syracuse because, in his own words, "I was ashamed lest I appear to myself as a pure theorist, unwilling to touch any practical task";[6] he failed dismally. Nevertheless, his students became important political leaders in numerous cities and even tutors of kings, as Aristotle was in Macedon, while the Academy provided a model for organizing the education of the Greek and later the Roman political elites that lasted to the end of antiquity.

However brilliant the models of the just society that Plato described in his two great works, the *Republic* and the *Laws*, they suffered from two crippling weaknesses that were shared by most Greek thinkers of his time. First, Plato could not conceive of any other framework for Greek society than the *polis* despite the fact that chronic tension between *poleis* was one of the principal causes of the problems of fourth-century

BCE Greece. Second, he and his contemporaries could not overcome one of the most pernicious legacies of the fifth century BCE: the belief that Greeks and "barbarians" were natural enemies between whom war was always just and that Persia was the quintessential barbarian enemy. These two problems combined to blind the Greeks until it was too late to the reality that the real threat to them and their way of life was not their old eastern enemy, Persia, but a new northern enemy, the kingdom of Macedon.

Located on the frontier between the Greeks and the Thracians and other north and west Balkan peoples, Macedon faced threats from all sides. Like its far-eastern contemporary, the kingdom of Qin, Macedon also was influenced culturally and socially by its neighbors—Greeks to the south and Thracians and Illyrians to the north and west—while chronic hostilities with those same neighbors fostered the development of a warrior ethos.

Little is known about early Macedonian history. Even whether the Macedonians were Greek is unclear, although linguistic evidence suggests that Macedonian was a Greek dialect. To the ancient Greeks, however, the Macedonians were just another group of unimportant barbarians, whose culture had nothing in common with their own and whose kings rarely died in bed. It is not surprising, therefore, that the Greeks didn't recognize the danger from Macedon until the kingdom had already emerged in the 350s BCE as the strongest military power in the Balkans.

The transformation of Macedon from a weak and unstable kingdom into the dominant military power in the Balkans was largely the work of Philip II, the father of Alexander the Great. During his twenty-four-year reign from 360 BCE to 336 BCE, Philip tamed the Macedonian aristocracy and reorganized the Macedonian army into a tightly disciplined infantry and cavalry force personally loyal to the king and used it to build an empire extending from Greece in the south to the Danube in the north, covering roughly the modern states of Greece, Albania, European Turkey, and Bulgaria. Loyalty depended, however, on Philip's ability to reward his aristocratic officers and troops, and only war could provide the necessary resources. Trapped by the logic of his own reforms, Philip already had launched an invasion of the Persian Empire, when his assassination in 336 BCE at his daughter's wedding threatened all his achievements with ruin.

That Macedon did not fall back into the old instability was due to his successor, his twenty-year-old son Alexander. Although he succeeded to a kingdom facing civil war at home and rebellion by its

This silver medallion, which was minted around 325 for distribution to Alexander's troops during or shortly after his Indian campaign, depicts the king holding the thunderbolt of Zeus and a royal scepter. On the reverse side, Alexander appears as a cavalryman attacking the Indian king Porus, who rides on an elephant. The iconography of ancient coins conveyed political and cultural messages to their recipients, in this case celebrating Alexander's victory over his most formidable Indian opponent. © The Trustees of the British Museum/Art Resource, NY ART500354

non-Macedonian subjects, Alexander not only survived against all expectations, but during his thirteen-year reign from 336 to 323 BCE he also carried Macedonian arms all the way to western India and completed the conquest of the Persian Empire that had been begun by Philip.

Alexander's conquest of the Persian Empire was as remarkable as the campaigns of Cyrus II that had led to its foundation two centuries earlier. Most of the credit belongs to Alexander's extraordinary tactical and strategic skills and the exceptional fighting ability of his troops. Luck also played a big role as political instability caused by conflict over the royal succession undermined Persian efforts to mount an effective resistance to Alexander's invasion.

Alexander died prematurely at the age of thirty-three, so his legacy was essentially negative; he destroyed the Persian Empire, ending its rule of western Asia that had brought stability and prosperity to the region for more than two centuries. The task of establishing a new political order in the vast territories conquered by Alexander fell to his successors, men to whom the millennia-old cultural traditions of the ancient civilizations they now ruled were profoundly alien. Historians call the new order they shaped the Hellenistic or "Greek-like" world, but that slightly derogatory designation understates the richness and diversity of its achievements.

One thing, however, is not in dispute. The process by which the new political order emerged was long and violent. On his deathbed Alexander is supposed to have prophesied that his empire would go "to the best man; for I foresee that my friends will fight great funeral games over my body."[7] He was a good prophet. Four decades of bitter civil war among Alexander's generals between 323 and 281 BCE, during which the Macedonian royal family was destroyed, were required before a new state system took shape in the former territories of the Persian Empire. In place of the unified polity that was the Persian Empire three great kingdoms ruled by Macedonian dynasties dominated the vast territory from the Mediterranean to the borders of India: the Ptolemies in Egypt, the Seleucids in the Near and Middle East, and the Antigonids in Macedon. These three kingdoms provided the framework for political and cultural life in western Asia for almost two centuries until the advance of Rome in the west and Parthia in the east put an end to the world created by Alexander's conquests.

The Greeks were the principal beneficiaries of these changes. Almost immediately after Alexander's death in the summer of 323 BCE his generals abandoned his policy of appointing Persians to high offices. As a result, the Greeks and their culture came to occupy a privileged place in the new order. Instead of being citizens of tiny *poleis* scattered around the Mediterranean and Black Seas like frogs living on the shore of a fish pond, in Plato's vivid phrase,[8] they became an integral part of the political elite of the new Macedonian kingdoms. Throughout their vast territories a simplified form of Greek called *koine*—the common language—gradually replaced Aramaic as the language of government and trade and a Greek education became the indispensable mark of social prestige and influence. As a result a person could travel from the Mediterranean to India knowing only Greek. Greek history had become part of the mainstream of world history, and Greek culture became one of the few cultures to significantly influence the cultures of other peoples living beyond the borders of the countries of their origin.

At first glance, this evidence suggests that the new Macedonian kingdoms were segregated societies, but the reality was different. Like Alexander, the Ptolemies and Seleucids viewed their kingdoms as their personal property because they consisted of "land that had been won by the spear." Also like Alexander, they ruled as autocrats with the assistance of their "companions," men who originally were recruited from their relatives and friends, to whom they assigned whatever posts and tasks they wished. Over time, however, as the size and scope of their governments increased, terms like "friend" and "kinsman" became titles indicating high government office rather than descriptors of real relationships to the king. Outside their courts, however, the Macedonian kings followed Alexander's example and retained much of the administrative and economic infrastructure that had existed under the Persians. Most important, the new Macedonian kings relied on the cooperation of the same local and priestly elites who had served Alexander and the Persians before him to manage local affairs.

For the kings this situation meant that like their Persian predecessors they had to play differing roles for the multiethnic populations of their kingdoms: traditional Macedonian kings for their Macedonian and Greek subjects and Babylonian kings or pharaohs for their native subjects. Evidence of this royal role-playing is abundant. Egyptian artists portrayed the Ptolemies as pharaohs and Greek heroes. Royal benefactions and victories were celebrated in Greek and hieroglyphic inscriptions in Egypt, and Greek and cuneiform inscriptions in Mesopotamia. Most important of all, the Ptolemies and Seleucids actively fulfilled the principal duty of ancient kings, maintaining peace with the gods by building both Greek and non-Greek temples, performing the traditional rituals, and providing the temples and their priests with the resources required to perform appropriately the rituals and sacrifices the gods demanded.

In implementing this program, however, they faced one fundamental problem: demography. Quite simply, there were not enough Macedonians and Greeks to fulfill the roles assigned to them in the new kingdoms. The Ptolemies and Seleucids inherited Alexander's surviving veterans, but their numbers were limited. Immigration partially filled the gap, but the immigrants were mainly soldiers and, therefore, largely male; and in any event, the scale of immigration declined during the course of the third century BCE. Intermarriage solved part of the problem, but the inevitable result was that over time more and more so-called Greeks were, in fact, assimilated non-Greeks, who assumed a Greek identity because of the opportunities it offered, a process that was all the easier because increasingly Greek identity became a matter of education instead of birth.

Social change, however, was not limited to issues of identity. The spread of a Greek lifestyle in the new kingdoms brought with it the expansion of the use of slaves in households and the economy as a whole. At the same time, at least in Egypt, where papyri recovered from trash

The Rosetta Stone contains three versions of a decree inscribed in hieroglyphic and demotic Egyptian and in Greek; the decree was issued by a general meeting of the chief priests of Egypt to celebrate the coronation of Ptolemy V as king of Egypt in 196 BCE. It illustrates the collaboration between the Macedonian king and the priesthood that was essential to maintaining Macedonian rule in Egypt. Shutterstock 230498917

dumps and mummy wrappings provide insight into daily life, opportunity for elite Greek women clearly increased as they gained access for the first time to education. Equally important, by taking advantage of Egyptian law with its recognition of women's ability to act in their own name, they gained the right to control their own property and conduct business without the need to rely on the goodwill of a male guardian. Unfortunately, the surviving evidence does not reveal whether Greek women in the Seleucid kingdom took advantage of the similar privileges allowed women in Babylonian law.

The result of these changes was a social and cultural revolution that slowly but steadily spread through the territory of the former Persian Empire and alienated much of the native elite from their own societies and their traditional cultures. Not surprisingly, there was resistance to the new Greek-dominated order. Some examples were personal, as exemplified by the Macedonian religious recluse who complained to a government official that his Egyptian neighbors "forced their way in [to the shrine where he lived] with the intention of dragging me out and driving me away ... despite the fact that I am a Greek."[9] Some rebellions convulsed whole societies, like the uprising that restored native rule to Upper Egypt for two decades at the end of the third century BCE and the Jewish revolt in the 160s BCE that frustrated the Seleucid king Antiochus IV's attempt to suppress Judaism that Jews still celebrate in the festival of Chanukah. The relative success of these revolts, however, was the exception, not the rule. More typical were conditions in the new cities, like Alexandria, that Alexander and his successors founded from Egypt to India.

Alexandria was the first and most renowned of these new cities and the site of Alexander the Great's tomb. The first three Ptolemies transformed it into the foremost city of the Hellenistic world with a multiethnic population that ultimately reached half a million people and included Macedonians, Greeks, Egyptians, and a large and vibrant Jewish community. The clearest symbol of the dynamism and originality of Hellenistic Alexandria was its signature monument, the Pharos. Built by the architect Sostratus of Cnidus for Ptolemy II, the Pharos was the first skyscraper, a three-hundred-foot-high polygonal tower topped by a statue of Zeus Soter ("Savior") whose beacon fire, reflected far out to sea by mirrors, guided ships to Alexandria, bringing goods to the city from the whole world known to the Greeks.

Alexandria was a cosmopolitan city. Most obvious were its Greek aspects such as its grid-style street plan and the Ptolemies' two great cultural foundations: the research center known as the Museum, where distinguished scholars, supported by government stipends, conducted research in science and Greek literature, and the royal library, which was intended to contain copies of every book written in Greek, a collection that ultimately reached seven hundred thousand papyrus rolls. Discoveries in its cemeteries and in the remains of the royal quarter, now sunk under water in Alexandria's harbor, however, indicate that the city had a mixed culture. It turns out that the Ptolemies decorated the Pharos and filled their capital with Egyptian art and that upper-class Greeks were buried in tombs that combined Greek and Egyptian rituals and iconography. And Alexandria was not unique, since archaeology has revealed a similar mix of Greek and non-Greek architectural styles at Ai Khanum in Bactria at the other end of the Hellenistic world.

Greek culture flourished in the new kingdoms. Indeed, some of the greatest masterpieces of Greek literature and art were created in the three centuries that followed the death of Alexander the Great, while new philosophies such as Epicureanism and Stoicism, whose teachings emphasized how individuals might achieve self-sufficiency in a chaotic world, flourished. A central feature of Greek culture in the Hellenistic period, however, was the development of an educational system based on the major writers of archaic and classical Greece that was accessible to both Greeks and non-Greeks. Just as they did in connection with the *Vedas* in India and the five Confucian classics in China, scholars created new disciplines such as grammar in order to establish sound texts of the Homeric epics and other classical writers, identify their authentic works, and explain obscure allusions in them and the peculiarities of their language. As a result, these works remained intelligible and continued to function as models for contemporary writers.

The spread of Greek education to non-Greeks produced dramatic results. As the ancient scribal traditions of Egypt and Babylonia ceased to be the gateway to profitable government careers, their attractiveness to native elites waned, leading to their inevitable decline. At the same time the Greek view of the world they inhabited became contested ground as non-Greek intellectuals such as the Egyptian Manetho and the Babylonian Berossus composed histories of their peoples in Greek but based on native sources. Greek translations of native texts also appeared. The most spectacular and, ultimately, the most influential was the Septuagint, the Greek translation of the Hebrew scriptures, which resulted from an initiative of Ptolemy II and became the fundamental source book about Judaism for early Christians.[10]

Particularly lively, however, was the cultural interaction in science. Although virtually every area of scientific study was affected, two examples will illustrate the phenomenon. Access to the corpus of Babylonian astronomical observations enabled the early second-century BCE mathematician and astronomer Hipparchus to create a star map that was incorporated into the *Almagest* of the second-century CE scholar Ptolemy and remained standard in Islamic and European astronomy until the scientific revolution. At the same time the expansion of trade enriched the pharmacopeia of the Greeks with new drugs from Egypt,

Mesopotamia, and India. Even religion was affected as Egyptian cults such as those of Isis and Osiris, Judaism, Mesopotamian astrology, and even Buddhism adapted to accommodate the needs of new Greek adherents.

Although the establishment of the Macedonian kingdoms brought with it remarkable changes in the social and cultural life of ancient Eurasia, the political influence of these kingdoms remained largely confined to the territory of their Persian predecessor, and then not to all of it. Dynasties descended from the old Persian aristocracy continued to rule extensive territories in the west including Armenia and much of central and northern Anatolia, while in the east Macedonian rule in northwest India did not survive the fourth century BCE.

It was not supposed to be this way. At the end of his reign Alexander was planning to invade Arabia, and plans for campaigns in the west against Carthage and Italy were found in his papers after his death. Although the feasibility of these campaigns was already debated in antiquity, that does not matter, since Alexander's future plans were cancelled by his officers and troops immediately after his death at Babylon in the summer of 323 BCE. The reach of the Macedonian kingdoms' economic and cultural influence was far greater, however. Greek-style trade goods are found from north Africa and Spain in the west to deep into central Asia in the east and from southern Arabia and Nubia in the south to the Eurasian steppes in the north. The work of Greek craftsmen and artists spread over the same area, while the urban design and architecture of non-Greek cities echoed that of Alexandria and Antioch and the other new cities built by Alexander and his successors.

The result was a paradox. On the one hand, the influence of Greek culture extended far beyond the borders of the Macedonian kingdoms, becoming a sort of cultural *lingua franca*. Non-Greek rulers—Thracian, Iranian, and even Jewish—issued coins with Greek-style portraits, patronized Greek temples, sought honors from Greek cities, and boasted that they were philhellenes, friends of the Greeks. On the other hand, the cancellation of Alexander's planned future campaigns meant that the political history of states beyond the borders of the Macedonian kingdoms followed independent trajectories.

Ties with the Macedonian kingdoms were closest with states on their immediate periphery. In the Arabian peninsula the four south Arabian kingdoms prospered by controlling the incense trade to the Mediterranean and western Asian states and functioning as middlemen in the sea-borne commerce between south Asia and the Near East and northeast Africa. Across the Red Sea in the upper Nile Valley, Kush also prospered, providing Ptolemaic Egypt with African goods ranging from slaves to exotic animals and ivory; it used its new wealth to adorn its capital Meroe and other sites with temples that echoed contemporary Egyptian models. At the same time, the third-century BCE Ptolemies were trying to find an African source of war elephants to counter their Seleucid rivals' monopoly on Indian elephants, meaning that relations between Egypt and Kush became particularly close. The result was a political and cultural revolution in Kush led by kings with close ties to the Ptolemies. Local deities like the royal war god Apedemak gained new prominence. Egyptian also was replaced as the language of government by the native Meroitic language written in a new alphabetic script that was easier to learn than the Egyptian hieroglyphs that had been used since the foundation of the kingdom six centuries earlier.

By contrast, the central and western Mediterranean and continental Europe were almost separate worlds. Trade ties with the Aegean and Macedonian kingdoms were close, and fashions from the eastern Mediterranean spread westward. Throughout the region Greek and Greek culture became important parts of aristocratic life, but they didn't become the keys to social prominence and government service as they had in the east. Instead, they were integrated into local cultures, producing vigorous hybrids in which native values were expressed in Greek forms such as, for example, the Roman epic, which melded Roman historical themes and Homeric style.

Their lack of involvement in the conflicts of the eastern Mediterranean did not, of course, mean that the states of the central and western Mediterranean were at peace. Quite the contrary, during the fourth and early third centuries BCE, Carthage and Rome, the two principal powers in the region, consolidated their power. Carthage tightened its hold on the Mediterranean islands and north Africa from Tunisia to the Atlantic, while Rome crushed the Etruscans and the Samnites and united all Italy from the Po Valley to Sicily into a formidable military federation, thereby setting the stage for a century-long confrontation that would decisively change the framework of political and cultural life in western Eurasia for the rest of antiquity.

Conditions were more complicated in Europe north of the Alps. The trade routes that brought continental goods ranging from metals to amber, animal hides, and slaves to the south and Mediterranean goods including wine, luxury metal wares, and coins to the north continued to function. Rapidly increasing population, however, filled up accessible arable land; this made it more difficult for ambitious warriors to gain status through building a personal following by rewarding warriors with the proceeds of successful raids. For some, the solution was mercenary service in the Mediterranean and western Asian empires, but for many the solution was migration, which would allow aspiring chieftains to carve out new territories for themselves and their followers.

The age of Celtic migrations lasted from the late fifth century BCE to the first half of the third century BCE. Celtic populations and the associated La Tene culture moved south over the Alps into northern Italy and southeast down the Danube valley to the western coasts of the Black Sea and ultimately to central Anatolia. To the writers and artists who created the surviving literary and visual images of the Celts, these people were fearsome warriors, who went into battle naked, collected heads, and practiced human sacrifice, all of which were true but not the whole story. Wherever they settled, hybrid cultures formed as La Tene traditions mixed with local cultures producing Celto-Etruscan cities in north Italy, Thracian- and Scythian-influenced Celtic cultures in eastern Europe and the western Black Sea steppe, and in Anatolia Hellenized Celtic kingdoms, the forerunners of the Galatians who St. Paul addressed in the first century CE.

The impact, both direct and indirect, of Alexander's conquests was not limited to western Eurasia. Equally revolutionary developments also occurred in south Asia at the eastern end of the Hellenistic world. While Alexander clearly hoped to maintain control of his conquests in western India, his organization of the Indian satrapies of his empire proved inadequate so that the Macedonian presence in India had disappeared by the end of the fourth century BCE.

In an understandable reaction against the exaggerated importance that historians of the British Raj ascribed to Alexander, Indian nationalist historians maintain that Alexander's invasion was only a violent episode with no long-term significance for Indian history, but this is also an exaggeration. Although Alexander created little in India that survived his life, his campaign did have a significant impact on the course of Indian history. Specifically, by destabilizing much of western India and the Punjab, Alexander created a political space that local Indian rulers rushed to fill. The most successful of those rulers was Chandra Gupta Maurya. During his almost three-decade-long reign from 326 BCE to 297 BCE, he took advantage of the chaotic situation in northwest India after Alexander's death to carve out a small kingdom; it served as a base from which his forces swept across the north Indian plain and overthrew the kingdom of Magadha in the Ganges Valley, thereby laying the foundation for the first Indian empire and ultimately changing the course of south Asian, and eventually central and east Asian history.

Although Chandra Gupta's fame as a great ruler and conqueror lasted into late antiquity, little is known of his life. Indian sources characterize him alternately as a member of the Kshatriya Varna and heir to the throne of Magadha and a Shudra who died as a Jain monk, while Greek tradition portrays him as an admirer and successor of Alexander. What is clear, however, is that by 305 BCE Chandra Gupta had brought all of north India under his control and was strong enough to force Seleucus I to sign a treaty in which he ceded all Macedonian territory in northwest India and agreed to a marriage alliance with the Indian king in exchange for five hundred war elephants and their drivers and trainers and recognition of Seleucid control of Bactria.

With his western frontier secured by an alliance with Seleucus I, Chandra Gupta could concentrate on organizing his kingdom and transforming the former Nanda capital of Pataliputra into a great city on the scale of Alexandria in the west. As a result, the center of Indian culture shifted from the Indus River valley to the Ganges River valley where it would remain for the rest of antiquity. The Maurya Empire reached its peak, however, during the reign of Chandra Gupta's grandson, Ashoka, whose realm included most of south Asia from northwest India to south of the Deccan plateau, while his diplomatic ties extended from the Aegean in the west to Nepal, south India, and Sri Lanka in the east. Little was known about Ashoka until nineteenth-century European scholars deciphered his remarkable inscriptions, providing unique insight into his response to the realities of imperial rule:

> The Kalinga country was conquered by King Priadarsi, Beloved of the Gods, in the eighth year of his reign. One hundred and fifty thousand persons were carried away captive, one hundred thousand were slain, and many times that number died.... The Beloved of the Gods, conqueror of the Kalingas, is moved to remorse now. For he has felt profound sorrow and regret because the conquest of a people previously unconquered involves slaughter, death, and deportation.[11]

The result of Ashoka's personal experience of the violence of conquest was twofold. As king, he adopted an ideology of rule based on toleration of all religions and non-violence toward both peoples and animals that he called the *Dharma*, the Way. Ashoka promulgated the *Dharma* throughout his empire in a remarkable series of inscriptions composed in the various languages of his subjects—Greek and Aramaic in the northwest and Prakrit in the central core—and made its enforcement the central duty of the officials of his government. Personally, he converted to Buddhism.

Like the fourth-century CE Roman emperor Constantine, Ashoka believed that as king he had the right to play an active role in his new religion, patronizing the Council of Pataliputra in ca. 250 BCE where the canon of the authentic works of the Buddha was determined. He also ordered the expulsion of dissident monks and nuns from the Buddhist order, and built stupas—monuments supposedly containing relics of the Buddha that were the foci of pilgrimage—throughout his empire. He even dispatched missionaries to spread knowledge of his *Dharma* to neighboring countries including Sri Lanka in the south and the Macedonian kingdoms in the west and arranged everywhere "for two kinds of medical treatment, treatment for men and for animals."[12] Unfortunately, we have no information concerning the reception Ashoka's missionaries received in the Greek world, but an important result of the establishment of permanent ties between Maurya India and the Greco-Macedonian west was a revolutionary change in the Greek and later Roman understanding of India.

Although knowledge of India expanded throughout the Hellenistic period, the most important contribution to the new understanding of Indian society and culture was made by Megasthenes, ambassador of Seleucus I to the court of Chandra Gupta. While the book Megasthenes wrote about India is lost, Greek and Roman geographers and historians relied on it for information about India throughout the rest of antiquity and, their summaries make it still a major source of information concerning ancient India. Thanks to Megasthenes's work, the dominant Greek and Roman view of India came to be that of an enormous country ruled by a centralized monarchy in which people's places in society were determined by the caste into which they were born instead of a land filled with fantastic monsters like dog-headed people, as had been believed before Alexander the Great's invasion.

The direct impact of Alexander's conquests, however, did not extend beyond south Asia. Like the far west, so also the far east remained virtually a separate world with only loose ties to the rest of Eurasia, and as before, it was war that drove developments in China in the fourth and third centuries BCE.

The Warring States Period was well named. By one scholar's count there were 358 wars between the late sixth century BCE and the early third century BCE,[13] a level of interstate violence virtually unprecedented in world history. Not surprisingly, the guiding purpose of the seven major kingdoms that dominated north and central China was raising the largest and most effective armies for the seemingly endless wars they fought. What was new in the fourth and third centuries BCE, however, was that the goal of war changed from victory in battle to total destruction of the enemy and annexation of his territory. Exemplary of the new approach to warfare was the action of Qin general Bai Qi, who, it was claimed, buried alive 400,000 captured soldiers after his decisive victory over the kingdom of Zhao in 260 BCE, thereby eliminating the last rival to the emergence of Qin as the most powerful kingdom in north China.

Continuous war forced changes in the social and political systems of the kingdoms but most dramatically in Qin, where the fourth-century BCE reformer Shang Yang pushed through a thorough reorganization of the kingdom's legal and tax structure aimed at maximizing its military potential through strengthening its agricultural base. Henceforth, the foundation of Qin society was an agricultural unit consisting of a nuclear family, all of whose male members were conscripted to military service and whose position in society was determined by the rank they achieved based on the number of enemy heads they collected in battle. At the same time, the final disappearance of the hereditary aristocracy that had dominated battle under the Zhou left no buffer between the mass of the population and the increasingly autocratic kings and the bureaucracies through which they ruled their kingdoms.

The extraordinary violence of the Warring States Period also led to fundamental changes in Chinese intellectual life. As in contemporary Greece, Chinese philosophers strove to find a solution to the crisis. Suggestions varied widely but all agreed on the irrelevance of the Confucian ideal of governance by reliance on example informed by the values of the Zhou aristocracy. At one extreme were the Daoists, whose wise men sought salvation through a return to the perfection of the Dao, the original order of the world, and the rejection of the artificialities of civilization. The Daoist attitude to the "unnatural" character of civilization is well illustrated by a passage in the *Chuang Tzu*, in which a wise man asks if a captured tortoise "had been allowed to choose between dying and having its bones venerated for centuries to come or going on living with its tail dragging in the mud, which would it have preferred?" and receives the answer that "it would have preferred to go on living with its tail dragging in the mud."[14] The most influential of the Warring States schools of thought, however, were the Legalists, whose view that government should be based on the clear and consistent rule of law undergirded the reforms of Shang Yang:

> [The king] demands that what comes after shall match what went before, [and] governs the masses according to the law.... If he can make certain that men do not receive any unearned rewards nor

overstep their authority, that death penalties are justly handed out and no crime goes unpunished, then evil and malicious men will find no opening to carry out their private schemes.[15]

Connections between the Chinese kingdoms and the peoples of central Asia also became significantly closer during the Warring States Period. The discovery of Chinese and Iranian luxury goods in the frozen tombs at Pazyryk in southern Siberia and the appearance of Scythian animal motifs in Chinese art attest to trade relations across China's northern frontier. What drove Chinese interest in central Asia was the desire for horses for the cavalry that played an increasingly important role in the wars of the fourth and third centuries BCE. At the same time, the transformation of pasture into farmland to support the agricultural expansion demanded by Legalist reforms led to growing tension between Qin and the peoples of the steppe, setting the stage for the conflicts with nomad states like that of the Xiongnu that were to dominate much of the rest of China's history.

The fourth and third centuries BCE were a period of upheaval throughout Eurasia. Within a little over a century, political and cultural life changed radically. The most far-reaching changes were in western Asia where the disappearance of the Persian Empire marked the beginning of the end of political and cultural structures that had lasted for almost three millennia. Similar if not as dramatic changes also occurred in south and east Asia. New intellectual and religious traditions appeared, which would dominate elite education for the rest of antiquity spread through the region. At the same time, trade ties expanded, linking the major states with each other as well as peoples and states beyond their peripheries, laying the foundation for the increasingly globalized economy of the second and first centuries BCE and the early centuries CE.

CHAPTER 5

The Rise of the Peripheries: Rome and China

(ca. Third–Second Centuries BCE)

In 128 BCE, an emissary of the Han emperor Wu Di named Zhang Qian arrived in Bactria.[1] His journey had been long and hard. For most of the ten years it took, he had been a prisoner of the Xiongnu, the most powerful nomadic state in central Asia, even marrying a Xiongnu woman, who fled with him when he escaped. What he found when he finally reached Bactria astonished him. In the report on his experiences that Zhang Qian presented to Wu Di two years later, he described Bactria as a populous and prosperous region divided among a series of city-states that were subject to the Yuezhi[2] federation located north of the Oxus River, the modern Amu Darya. In the cities' market places he found goods from much of central Asia and even China, clear evidence that trade already existed between Bactria and China. Most remarkable, however, there was no trace of the Macedonian or Greek domination of Bactria that had resulted from Alexander's conquest two centuries earlier.

Zhang Qian's mission had been to negotiate an alliance between China and the Xiongnu's principal rival and enemy, the Yuezhi. In that he had failed, so he probably would not have been impressed to learn that his report marked a significant milestone in the historiography of world history. For the first time historians from both ends of Eurasia referred to the same series of events: the end of Greco-Macedonian rule in central Asia. The Seleucid kingdom, which had once ruled the enormous territory between western Asia and Bactria, had shrunk to little more than a Syrian kingdom, its former territories parceled out among a number of successor states of which the most important was the Parthian Empire, which ruled Iran and Mesopotamia. At the same time, as Zhang Qian's observations indicated, Bactria had become the hub of a vast trading system linking central Asia westward to the Mediterranean and southward to India. Although the volume of the trade probably still was not large, the foundation had been laid for the Silk Roads that would play so important a role in the commerce of late ancient and medieval Eurasia.

The roots of the collapse of the Seleucid kingdom lay almost two centuries in the past when Ptolemy I annexed Syria-Palestine with the Phoenician ports that were the *termini* of the important caravan routes linking the Mediterranean to southern Arabia and Mesopotamia and the Persian Gulf. The six so-called Syrian Wars the Seleucid kings fought with Ptolemaic Egypt over control of the Levant during the third century BCE combined with repeated conflicts over the royal succession drained the kingdom's resources and left it unable to respond effectively to threats to its Iranian and central Asian territories.

The critical moment came in 247 BCE when an Iranian-speaking nomadic people called the Parni seized control of a small but strategic territory southeast of the Caspian Sea, thereby founding the kingdom of Parthia and cutting Seleucid connections with Bactria, making possible its successful revolt a decade later. Although Antiochus III succeeded in briefly restoring Seleucid authority in Parthia and Bactria in the late third century BCE, his crippling defeat by the Romans in 190 BCE in the battle of Magnesia rendered his achievement ephemeral, creating the conditions that led to the situation that Zhang Qian found in Bactria three quarters of a century later. The Seleucid legacy survived, however, since the successor states of the Seleucid kingdom were built on foundations laid by the dynasty. As a result, Greeks and Greek culture continued to play an important role in the vast area between the Mediterranean and the border of India, but the nature of that role varied from region to region. Not surprisingly, however, Seleucid influence was weakest at the farthest frontier of their empire in Bactria. As successors of the Seleucids, the Greek kings of Bactria ruled a frontier kingdom bordering the Eurasian steppe that was constantly threatened by the nomadic peoples, who ultimately overwhelmed it in the 140s BCE, almost two decades before Zhang Qian's visit in 128 BCE.

The heart of Bactria was a series of cities founded by Alexander and his Seleucid successors like Ai Khanum near the Oxus River, whose remarkable ruins illuminated life in Hellenistic central Asia until the site was destroyed by looters during the Afghan civil wars of the late twentieth century. Superficially, Ai Khanum with its Greek-style mansions and theater would seem to have been a typical Greek city, but closer analysis reveals Iranian and Indian influence in the city's architecture and administration. At the same time, the increasing corruption of the legends on the Bactrian coinage indicates that knowledge of Greek steadily declined outside a small, educated elite during the kingdom's century-long existence.

The situation was more complex farther west in Parthia. Despite repeated Seleucid attacks, the Parthian kingdom survived and expanded from its core near the Caspian Sea to become the dominant power in western Asia. By the 140s BCE its territory encompassed all Iran and Mesopotamia, and its diplomatic and economic ties extended farther, reaching from the Mediterranean in the west to China in the east.

As their title King of Kings indicates, the Parthian kings ruled a loosely organized quasi-federal empire like their Persian predecessors. Also like the Persians, the Parthians retained much of their central Asian heritage. So the Parthian kings ruled with the support of an aristocracy, who served in peace as the king's councilors and in war as his elite cavalry; in return they received grants of landed estates, whose tenants produced their noble masters' agricultural wealth in peacetime and made up their military retinue in war.

As in Yuezhi-ruled Bactria, the Seleucid cities survived the Parthian conquest and continued to provide the core of the kingdom's administrative structure. Culturally, however, Parthian rule brought major changes. As the Parthian kings adopted the Iranian culture of the kingdom's heartland and the Greek culture of the Seleucid cities, this acceptance stripped the millennia-old, cuneiform-based culture of Mesopotamia of the government functions that had made knowledge of it prestigious and valuable. As a result, knowledge of the cuneiform script and the literature preserved in it shrank until both were limited to a few hereditary priestly and scribal families connected to temples in cities like Babylon and Uruk.

Even more complicated was the situation farther west in the Levant and Anatolia. Instead of the handful of powerful successor states like Parthia and Bactria that emerged in Iran and central Asia, the declining Seleucid kingdom gave way in the west to a plethora of small and medium-sized kingdoms, city-states, ethnic polities, and temple states. Of all these entities, however, the most remarkable was the kingdom of the Jews.

While the Jews' strict monotheism had set them apart from their neighbors as early as the beginning of the first millennium BCE, their distinctive social and political organization was the product of Persian

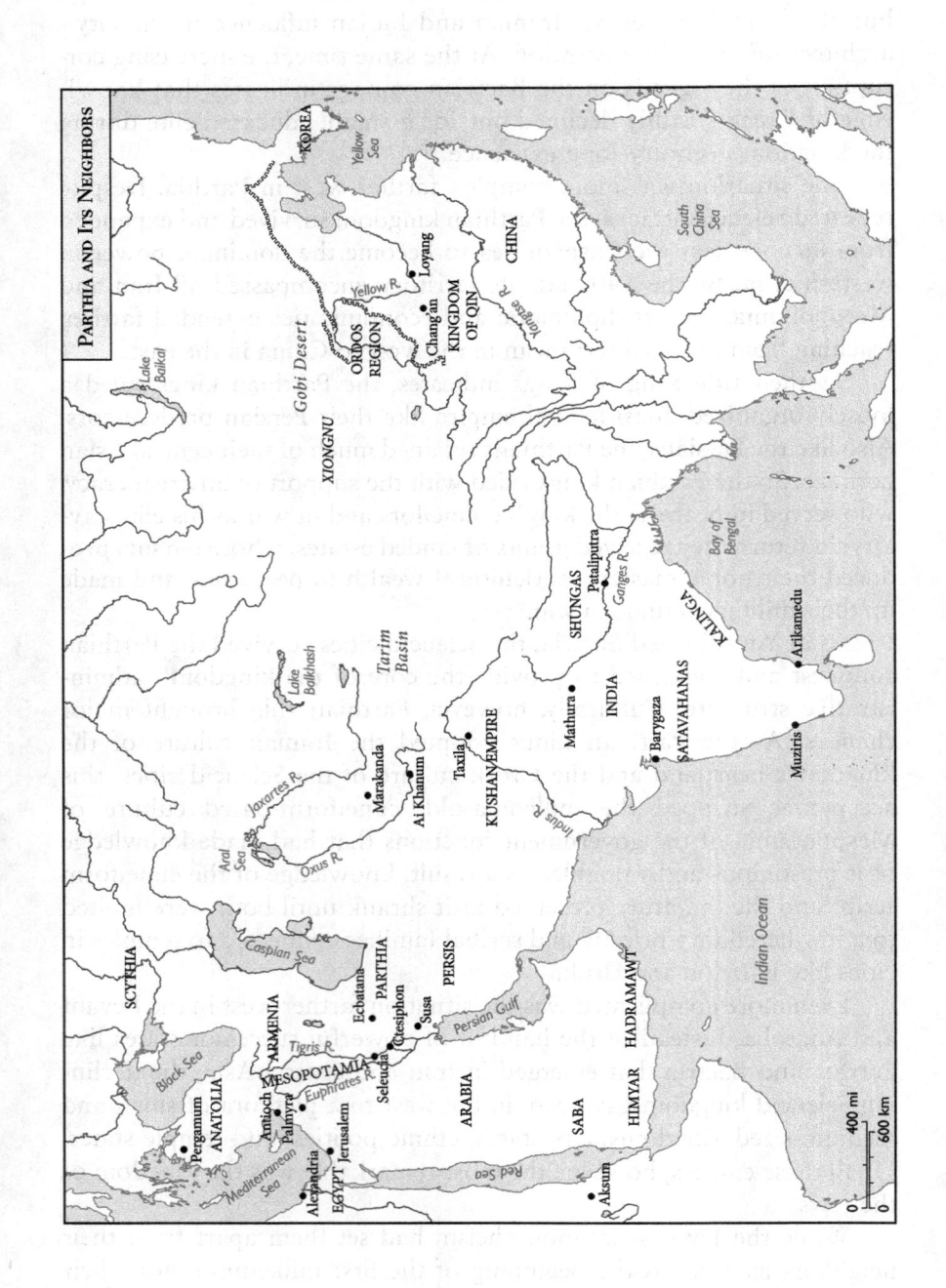

Parthia and Its Neighbors

rule. Although Jewish prophets held out the hope of the appearance of a messiah—a divinely anointed king—who would restore the glories of the Davidic kingdom, the Persians assigned the Jews the status of hereditary citizens of a temple state centered on the temple at Jerusalem and ruled by a hereditary priesthood, who governed according to ancestral law as embodied in the Torah, the first five books of the Bible. The Jewish temple state and the Jews' privilege of living according to the Torah survived the fall of the Persian Empire and the subsequent Macedonian conquest until the persecution of Antiochus IV provoked an uprising that led by the 140s BCE to the emergence of a Jewish kingdom that quickly became the most powerful military power in Syria-Palestine.

The new Jewish kingdom was not the kingdom hoped for by the prophets. As indicated by the Greek names of its kings and their agents and their surprising claim that the Jews were related to the Spartans, independence did not mean the end of Greek influence. Partly, this was pragmatism. In a world dominated by Greek-speaking states, Jewish kings needed agents able to function in such environments. And there are indications of significant Greek influence on the development of Hellenistic Judaism, shown by allusions to Greek literary works and philosophy by the authors of the Book of Judith and other books of the collection of books excluded from the Bible known as the Apochrypha.

Conflicts over how to reconcile the Greek-influenced culture of the Jewish kingdom with the Torah produced the rich and varied intellectual life in Judaea that we see in the New Testament, the works of the first-century CE Jewish historian Josephus, and the Dead Sea Scrolls. The variety of ideas about how to do this was great, but the most influential were those held by three groups: the Pharisees, scribes who advocated education and interpretation based on an oral Torah to keep the written Torah alive; the priestly Sadducees who argued for a literalism that permitted what was not explicitly prohibited; and ascetics like the Essenes who claimed that holy people should withdraw from society to await the appearance of the Messiah.

Zhang Qian found, therefore, virtually a new world when he traveled through central Asia in the early 120s BCE. Much, but not all, of the state system founded by Alexander's successors had disappeared. In particular, the cultural and economic links forged in those centuries survived and even expanded. Greek remained the primary *lingua franca* throughout the region, making possible continued communication and interchange of ideas between Greek and non-Greek intellectuals such as the mid-second-century BCE Babylonian astronomer Seleucus, who supported the heliocentric theory proposed by the Samian astronomer

Aristarchus a century earlier. Trade also grew with increased use of both the land routes through central Asia and the maritime route along the north coast of the Indian Ocean between south Asia, the Persian Gulf, and the Red Sea. In both cases the pioneers were not Greeks, however, but Arabs and central Asians in the north and Indians, Arabs, and possibly even southeast Asians in the south.

While cultural and economic ties survived the turmoil of the third and second centuries BCE and even flourished, the political order had collapsed. For the first time in four centuries no great empire governed the vast territory from the Mediterranean to the borders of India. Instead, power shifted to emerging new empires on the periphery of the former "center": Rome in the west and China in the east.

According to the historian Polybius, in 217 BCE a Greek politician warned his fellow Greeks that "if you ever allow the clouds now gathering in the west to loom over Greece, I deeply fear that all the games we now play with each other ... will be so thoroughly denied us that we shall find ourselves imploring the gods to grant us this right, to make war and peace with one another as we wish, and in general to manage our own internal disputes."[3] The Greeks could be pardoned for not taking the warning seriously. Rome was embroiled in the second of the three great wars it fought with its chief rival for domination in the western Mediterranean, the north African city of Carthage.

Rome and its great enemy had much in common, a fact already recognized in antiquity by political theorists and by some Greek historians who even claimed that the two cities were founded in the same year, 814 BCE. Although both had constitutions similar to those of Greek *poleis* with assemblies, advisory councils, and elected magistrates, they actually were aristocratic republics dominated by a small number of noble families who had overthrown the monarchies that had originally founded the cities. Both also had built regional empires, but there the similarities ended. While the nucleus of Rome's Italian empire was a federation of city-states whose extensive manpower was the true basis of Roman power, the core of Carthage's empire was a handful of Phoenician cities located in north Africa and the Mediterranean islands, so that the city's military power depended primarily on its navy and mercenaries recruited from its north African allies and the Iberians and Celts of Spain and Gaul.

Rome and Carthage would fight almost to the death in two of the longest and most brutal wars—the First and Second Punic Wars—in the history of Western antiquity; however, this conflict was not inevitable. The first-century BCE Roman epic poet Virgil recognized this in his great epic on the founding of Rome, the *Aeneid*; in it, he traced the origin of their hostility not to fundamental differences between the two cities but to a frustrated love affair between their legendary founders, the Trojan refugee Aeneas and the betrayed Phoenician princess Dido, who cursed Aeneas's Roman progeny with eternal hostility:

> That is my prayer, my final cry—I pour it out
> With my own lifeblood. And you, my Tyrians,
> Harry with hatred all his line, his race to come:
> Make that offering to my ashes, send it down below.
> No love between our peoples, ever, no pacts of peace![4]

Carthage was, in fact, Rome's first important overseas ally; the earliest treaty between them was signed in 509 BCE, the year of the founding of the Roman Republic, and the last in 279 BCE, a little over a decade before the outbreak of the First Punic War in 264 BCE. Complementary interests accounted for the long survival of the alliance. Carthage wanted security for its north African empire and its commerce and Rome desired guarantees against interference with its Italian allies and subjects. Roman expansion in south Italy, which threatened Carthaginian interests in Sicily, however, fundamentally changed the situation so that almost any spark could set off a conflagration. That spark was struck in 264 BCE, when the Romans crossed into Sicily to defend a rogue company of Italian mercenaries called the Mamertines—"Sons of [the war god] Mars"—against the Carthaginians, who had responded to pleas from the Greek cities of Sicily for relief from their depredations.

The First and Second Punic Wars were fought on a truly epic scale—the first lasting for twenty-three years from 264 BCE to 241 BCE and the second for sixteen years from 218 BCE to 202 BCE on battlefields ranging from Italy to Spain and north Africa. It is not surprising that one of the foundational works of Roman literature was an epic poem on the First Punic War, the *Bellum Punicum* of Gnaeus Naevius. Equally unsurprising is the fact that tales of heroic actions dominate ancient histories of the Punic Wars: the Roman general Regulus returning to Carthage to suffer death by torture after advising Rome not to accept Carthaginian peace terms in 256 BCE, the Carthaginian general Hannibal invading Italy by crossing the Alps in the winter of 218 BCE, Rome's remarkable rebound from her devastating defeat in the Battle of Cannae in 216 BCE, and the dramatic confrontation between Hannibal and Scipio Africanus, the two greatest generals of the age, in the final battle of the Second Punic War at Zama near Carthage in 202 BCE.

The results of the First and Second Punic Wars were equally dramatic. When peace was finally made in 202 BCE, political relations in the central and western Mediterranean had been transformed. Carthage had lost both its empire and the ability to defend itself against the ambitions of its former north African allies. Rome, on the other hand, emerged from the first two Punic Wars as the dominant power in the region with an enormous empire that included all of peninsular Italy and the Mediterranean islands of Sicily, Corsica, and Sardinia, and the former Carthaginian territories in Spain.

Almost immediately after the surrender of Carthage in 202 BCE, Rome turned its attention eastward, and in the next half century it extended its influence to cover the whole eastern Mediterranean basin. Not without justification, the Greek historian Polybius justified his choice of historical subject by rhetorically asking who would not "want to know how and thanks to what kind of political system almost the entire known world was conquered and brought under a single empire, the empire of the Romans, in less than fifty-three years?"[5] The story was a dramatic one, as Polybius well knew, having spent much of the first half of the second century BCE as a hostage in Rome to ensure the good behavior of his homeland, the Achaean League, one of the two federal states that dominated Greek politics.

Rome's expansion into the Greek world began with decisive victories over Macedon and the Seleucid king Antiochus III in the 190s BCE and the dramatic proclamation that the Romans had fought the kings to free the Greeks. It ended with the simultaneous destruction of Carthage and the ancient Greek city of Corinth and the annexation of Macedon in 146 BCE. The intervening years were marked by confusion and frustration on the part of both Rome and the Greeks and their eastern neighbors.

The root of the problem was in the Roman Senate. The Senate failed to understand that its policy of relying on pro-Roman oligarchies to uphold Roman interests with a minimum of direct Roman involvement in local affairs that had worked in Italy would not do so in Greece and the eastern Mediterranean, where freedom meant the right to pursue independent foreign policies. The result was that any sign of independence by the Greek cities or the various kings in the region roused Roman suspicions that were only assuaged by interventions intended to weaken the offending state. In the case of the Seleucid kingdom, for example, the Romans repeatedly supported breakaway groups such as the Jews or pretenders to the throne in order to prevent the possible emergence of another strong king such as Antiochus III. Even longtime

Roman allies might suffer the same fate if their actions seemed to threaten Roman interests. So, in 167 BCE the Greek city of Rhodes was threatened with war by the Roman Senate for daring to offer to serve as mediators between Rome and Macedon in the Third Macedonian War. The destructive cycle of Greek attempts to act independently followed by hostile Roman reactions continued until the disastrous events of 146 BCE finally disabused the peoples of the eastern Mediterranean of any remaining illusions about the Roman understanding of the meaning of freedom.

Roman imperial expansion in the third and second centuries BCE resulted in dramatic changes in the basic fabric of life in Italy whose effects would ripple throughout the Mediterranean basin during the rest of antiquity. The economic effects were most obvious. Aristotle defined war as a means of acquisition, and a century of almost ceaseless warfare poured an unprecedented amount of wealth into Italy in general and Rome in particular. The scale of loot, reparations, and tribute from Rome's enemies and subjects was so great that the Senate was even able to free Roman citizens permanently from all direct taxes. While much of the profits of empire swelled the wealth of the Roman aristocracy, enough remained to the Roman government to fuel an unprecedented building boom. Roads, temples, and aqueducts sprouted up throughout Italy, providing the infrastructure to support the growth of Rome into a metropolis of almost a million people, making it one of the largest cities in the world at this time. For the first time, Rome became a net importer of food as cheap grain imported from Sicily fed its surging population, swollen by immigrants from rural Italy displaced by the spread of commercial farms and huge ranches worked by slaves at the expense of small peasant holdings.

Economic change in antiquity was gradual, and its causes were often unclear to those who experienced them. The social and cultural effects of Rome's intrusion into the Greek east occurred quickly and were profound and long lasting. The poet Horace[6] summed them up in a famous line: "captive Greece took its iron captor captive and introduced the arts to crude Latium." When Horace wrote that line in the late first century BCE, the beginnings of Roman domination in Greece were more than a century in the past, and Greek influence had long been domesticated and was no longer controversial. Roman senators lived in splendid houses stuffed with Greek art, managed by Greek slaves and ex-slaves, spoke Greek fluently, employed Greek tutors to educate their children, and read books written in Latin such as Virgil's epic account of the foundation of Rome, the *Aeneid*, which required a thorough knowledge of Homer's *Iliad* and *Odyssey* to be fully appreciated.

While Horace knew the result of Greek influence on the development of Greek culture, second-century BCE Roman aristocrats experienced Hellenization as a virtual culture war; ideas that seemed subversive to them were flooding in from the Greek east, and they struggled to reconcile views, such as the Epicurean doctrine that pleasure was the primary good, with their traditional values, which stressed duty to family and the attainment of glory through service to the community in war and politics. Their reaction was extreme but understandable, since the impact was felt throughout Roman society, although most obviously in the vast growth in the number of Greek-speaking slaves. Conquest and sudden wealth fueled a huge slave trade—150,000 from one part of Greece in the year 168 BCE alone—that made such slaves ubiquitous in Rome, raising concerns among Roman traditionalists about corruption of the Roman citizen body.

And not just in the city. Slaves were an intimate part of Roman elite family life, managing Roman households, educating their children, preparing and serving their food, and serving them in the most intimate aspects of their lives including providing sexual services. Greek art—looted or bought—adorned the city and the great houses. Not surprisingly, Greek influence was blamed for every apparent threat to Roman values from the spread of subversive political ideas to the feminization of the Roman aristocracy and the unwillingness of upper-class Roman women to have enough children to replenish the Roman citizenry. Attempts repeatedly were made to limit the impact of Greek culture on Roman life ranging from the violent persecution of the cult of Bacchus—the Roman form of the Greek god Dionysus—in 186 BCE to the expulsion of teachers of rhetoric and a ban on the construction of permanent theaters in Rome, but Rome's continued imperial expansion in the Greek east frustrated all such efforts, as Horace recognized.

The revolutionary changes in the west that resulted from the collapse of the Seleucid kingdom were paralleled by contemporary developments in south Asia as the Seleucids' old ally, the Maurya Empire, gradually shrank back to its political core in the Ganges River Valley, thereby allowing its provinces to regain their former independence. The disappearance of the Maurya Empire opened the way to the emergence of a congeries of rival kingdoms covering the Indian peninsula from south India through the Deccan to the Punjab of which two were most important: a kingdom founded by a Bactrian Greek dynasty centered in northwest India, and the Shunga Empire located in the Ganges River Valley that was founded by a Brahman general named Pushyamitra, who murdered the last Maurya emperor around 184 BCE.

The overwhelmingly religious character of classical Indian literature means that little is known of the history of the century following the overthrow of the last Maurya emperor. However, war was endemic, and this is made clear by allusions in grammatical texts and dramas to various military events; the celebration of two horse sacrifices by Pushyamitra; the sack of Pataliputra, the Shunga capital, by the Indo-Greek king Menander; and a remarkable text, the Hathigumpha—Elephant Cave—inscription[7] which commemorates victories won by a first-century BCE king of Kalinga, Ashoka's old enemy, against states scattered all over central and north India. Not surprisingly, in view of the state of chronic warfare that gripped India in this period, the *Arthashastra*, the classic Indian treatise on statecraft, which reflects conditions in the second and first centuries BCE, describes the ideal king no longer as a promoter of *dharma* as Ashoka had done but as "the seeker after conquest ... who is endowed with the exemplary qualities both of the self and of material constituents [of the kingdom], and who is the abode of good policy."[8]

Ironically, the collapse of the Maurya Empire and the lack of a single powerful imperial state to replace it also stimulated cultural life as new centers of patronage emerged in the various successor states. As a result, changes in religious and literary culture occurred that would resonate up to the present. The most fundamental was the replacement of the vernacular languages known as Prakrits by Sanskrit, a formal literary language with a standardized grammar, as the dominant written language of India. As a result the foundation was laid for the development of a single religious and literary culture throughout south Asia that made possible the spread of Indian religion and culture through much of southeast Asia in the mid- and late first millennium CE. The original forms of numerous important Buddhist, Brahmanic, and Jain treatises were also composed in this period, although only the great grammatical study of Sanskrit by Patanjali is still extant. References in later works suggest, however, that included among the lost works were the sources of the authoritative synthesis of Brahmanic social thought known as the *Laws of Manu*; the classic political treatise, the *Arthashastra*; and the *Kama Sutra*, the standard Indian textbook of love for aristocratic young men.

The proliferation of sources of royal patronage also benefited religion, with the several major Indian religions finding support in different kingdoms: Buddhism in the Indo-Greek kingdoms, traditional Indian religion in the Shunga Empire, and Jainism in Kalinga. The results were evident in the construction of impressive religious monuments throughout India including the first permanent temples devoted to the worship of Indian deities, stupas where relics of the Buddha were preserved, and sanctuaries excavated into the sides of mountains. The nature of traditional Indian worship also changed as devotional cults appeared addressed to deities such as Vasudeva, the creator god Vishnu incarnate as Krishna, in addition to the sacrifices prescribed in the *Vedas*.

Economic activity also flourished. Buddhist tradition, for example, described Sagala, the capital of the Indo-Greek king Menander, as a "great center of trade" filled with "merchants, artisans, and shops of all kinds,"[9] while the Hathagumpha inscription refers to the construction of economically useful infrastructure including canals. Nor was this activity limited to India. As already mentioned, Indian merchants sailed to the Persian Gulf and southern Arabia, while the presence of Indian elephants in the Seleucid army as late as the 160s BCE indicates that the land routes to the west remained open.

While Rome was beginning the unification of the western periphery of Eurasia and the Maurya Empire was fragmenting, east Asia was also undergoing fundamental change. Polybius, the historian of Roman expansion, identified the 140th Olympiad, the four-year period from 220 BCE to 216, as the time when the integration of events throughout the Mediterranean and the Near East marked the beginning of world history. Although Polybius was perceptive in choosing the date for the beginning of his narrative, he could not have known that his Chinese counterpart, the first-century BCE Han historian Sima Qian, would have chosen almost the identical period as the beginning of Chinese imperial history. Specifically, he would have chosen the previous year, 221 BCE, when Ying Zheng, the king of Qin, completed a decade of whirlwind military campaigns during which he conquered the six surviving Warring States kingdoms—Han, Zhao, Yan, Wei, Chu, and Qi—and unified for the first time the valleys of the Yellow and Yangtze Rivers, the heartland of imperial China.

The decade between the foundation of the Qin Empire in 221 BCE and the first emperor's death in 210 BCE was foundational for the rest of Chinese history. Under his new name Huangdi, "Splendid Divinity," Ying Zheng fundamentally reorganized the political structure of China. Because the Han-period propaganda in the sources followed by Sima Qian portrayed the first emperor as a mad tyrant obsessed with dreams of immortality and violently hostile to Confucian scholars, it is not possible to reconstruct the personality of Ying Zheng. The main outlines of his reforms, however, are clear. As his name Huangdi indicates, the emperor was to be the link between the empire and heaven, assuring its goodwill during his life by performing sacrifices and after his death by the maintenance of his ancestor cult at the monumental tomb he had built for himself.

Appropriate to his central role in the earthly order, all government functions were believed to depend on the emperor's actions, and all officials, therefore, were his appointees and representatives. In practice, this meant that the kingdoms in the Warring States Period were suppressed and replaced by "commanderies" administered by royal officials. A vast system of roads of standardized width was also built to hold the empire together with a huge new capital city at Xianyang which was designed to be a microcosm of the empire and to serve as the administrative center for both the empire and the emperor's monumental tomb complex. True to legalist principles, which had informed Qin reforms since the fourth century BCE, a unified law code was issued for the empire, weights and measures were standardized, and agriculture was prioritized over all other economic activities. Unification was even extended into cultural life with standardization of the writing system and the drawing up of a list of approved texts to be taught to future officials in a new imperial academy. Less than a decade after his death in 210 BCE, however, all the first emperor's grandiose plans lay in ruins. His family had been murdered and his capital razed to the ground, destroyed in a series of empire-wide revolts. Of all his monumental creations only his tomb survived to still provide archaeologists and tourists with a vivid insight into his vision of the Qin Empire, or so it seemed.

Out of the wreckage a new dynasty—the Western Han—emerged, founded by the last surviving rebel against the Qin Dynasty, a commoner named Liu Bang; this dynasty would rule China for four centuries. The heart of resistance to Qin rule had been found politically in supporters of the restoration of the old Warring States kingdoms and culturally in Confucian scholars excluded from influence by the legalist advisors of the first emperor and his successors. After his victory, therefore, Liu Bang was forced to reward his most important followers with rule over ten kingdoms in eastern China and to extend royal patronage to Confucian scholars who redefined the curriculum of the imperial academy to emphasize the Confucian classics. In the western territories ruled by Liu Bang from his new capital at Chang'an in the old Qin center of the Wei River valley, however, the Qin system continued essentially unchanged. Not surprisingly, the principal political issue facing Liu Bang and his immediate successors was maintaining the unity of the empire against the separatist efforts of the rulers of the restored kingdoms, a struggle that lasted for half a century until their last rebellion was crushed in 154 BCE and the empire was reunited. Although the Han emperors publicly supported Confucian values, the basic institutional framework of the Han Empire could be described as a Qin legacy. It also was a Qin legacy that made relations with its central Asian neighbors the major issue in Han foreign affairs.

The origin of the Han opening to the west dates back to the Warring States Period. Technological and tactical innovations played a big part in the Warring States kingdoms' search for victory in their endless wars. Technological developments included inventions as complex as the crossbow and as basic as the wheelbarrow as well as improved iron metallurgy, which also led to improved agricultural yields and ultimately to the increased population necessary to provide the manpower for their armies. It was a tactical innovation, however, that turned China toward central Asia, namely, the replacement of chariotry, the weapon of choice of the Zhou aristocracy, by cavalry.

The adoption of cavalry by Warring States armies resulted in the final eclipse of the military significance of the old Zhou aristocracy; the creation of a profitable trade in horses between Chinese kingdoms and central Asian nomads, who alone could supply the horses the kingdoms needed for their new cavalry units; and the annexation by the kingdoms of territory inhabited by the nomads for the pasture needed to support the cavalry horses. The process reached its peak during the reign of the first emperor, who annexed the Ordos Plateau which was the territory enclosed by the great bend of the Yellow River, moved in settlers to work the land, and used the labor of his soldiers to defend it by linking up boundary walls built by his predecessors into a single monumental defensive wall 2,584 miles long. Although the Qin wall was not a stone construction like the existing Great Wall, its construction required tremendous effort and presented a major threat to the interests of the Xiongnu. In response to the pressure of Qin expansion, the Xiongnu rallied in the early second century BCE to the leadership of a charismatic ruler named Modun.

According to the Chinese historian Sima Qian, Modun became the Xiongnu paramount leader—the *Shanyu*—by training his followers to follow his orders without question by forcing each one to commit a series of outrageous acts: first, killing his favorite horse, then his favorite concubine, and finally his father. Whatever the truth of the story of Modun's rebellion, once he became *Shanyu*, he rapidly built the earliest attested nomadic empire in central Asia, an empire that ultimately included the whole area between western Manchuria in the north and Mongolia and the oasis towns of the Tarim basin in the south. The ramifications of the creation of the Xiongnu Empire were felt throughout central Asia. In the west, for example, repeated defeats inflicted on the Yuezhi forced them in the 170s BCE to begin their long march toward Bactria, where Zhang Qian found them in the early 120s BCE.

More remarkable was the reaction of the recently established Han Dynasty. Heavily defeated by the Xiongnu in 201 BCE in a battle in which Liu Bang barely escaped with his life, the Han government resigned itself to seeking a *modus vivendi* (a way of peaceful coexistence) with the Xiongnu. The result was the institution in the 180s BCE of the *Heqin* or "Peace and Kinship" policy in which the Han government recognized the Xiongnu Empire as a co-equal state. Under this policy, the Han would annually give the Xiongnu substantial payments of silk and various foodstuffs, the *Shanyu* would receive a Han princess as his wife, the Qin wall would be the border between the Xiongnu and Han empires, and the Xiongnu and Han were to be recognized as equal in rank.

Despite its humiliating character, the *Heqin* policy remained in force for almost half a century. Its rationale was that the gifts of Chinese goods and the royal princesses would encourage Xiongnu acculturation and make them more manageable. The sad fate of a consort of the Han emperor Yuandi named Wang Qiang, who voluntarily agreed to become the wife of the *Shanyu*, however, illustrates the failure of the policy to achieve its goals:

> Wang Qiang had a son, named Shiwei. When the *shanyu* died, Shiwei succeeded to the throne. The unusual custom with the Xiongnu is that when the father dies, the son takes his mother to wife. Wang Qiang asked Shiwei, "Are you a Chinese or a Xiongnu?"
> Shiwei answered, "I just want to be a Xiongnu." At this Wang Qiang swallowed poison and took her own life.[10]

Unintended results are the stuff of history. While the *Heqin* policy clearly failed to achieve its goals, much of the silk provided the Xiongnu under its terms was passed on by them to other peoples living farther west until ultimately some of it reached the Mediterranean, inspiring the demand for Chinese silk that would provide the basis for the development of the Silk Roads in the early centuries CE.

The basic framework of political and cultural history for the remainder of antiquity took shape during the hundred years between the mid-third and mid-second centuries BCE. Power shifted from the center to the peripheries, where new empires emerged, Rome in the west and Han China in the east, while in the north the first great nomadic states appeared in central Asia, the Xiongnu and their rival the Yuezhi. Economically, the new state system would eventually provide both the markets for exotic luxury goods and the stability that would make the long-distance trade in such goods possible. Culturally, imperial patronage of a limited number of *lingua francas* and standardized writing systems—Greek in west Asia and the Mediterranean, Sanskrit in south Asia, and Han Chinese in east Asia—facilitated the development and spread throughout Eurasia of new text-based cultural traditions and ultimately of "religions of the book" such as Christianity, Manicheism, Confucianism, and Buddhism.

CHAPTER 6

A New Order in Afro-Eurasia

(ca. Second Century BCE–Second Century CE)

In 98 BCE the Han emperor Wu Di condemned his Grand Astrologer Sima Qian to be castrated in the "Silk Worm Chamber." Sima Qian's alleged offense was defaming Wu Di by speaking in defense of a disgraced general named Li Ling, who had been sentenced to death for deserting to the Xiongnu after suffering a severe defeat.

Eunuchs were the personal attendants of the emperor and his family and therefore exercised great influence on government affairs. Nevertheless, eunuchs, whom Sima Qian bitterly described as "something left over from the knife," also were viewed with disgust in the patriarchal society of China. The honorable course for a government official condemned to castration like Sima Qian, therefore, was to commit suicide. Despite the pressure of tradition, however, he chose to live, although he was always aware that to the members of the royal court he was a "mere mutilated body dwelling in degradation."[1] His decision to live no matter the cost in personal humiliation ironically was caused by his desire to fulfill one of the primary obligations of Confucianism, filial piety, by completing the history of China begun by his father and predecessor as Grand Astrologer, Sima Tan.

The result of Sima Qian's refusal to do the "honorable thing" was one of the world's great histories, *The Records of the Grand Historian*. In the remaining twelve years of his life Sima Qian completed his father's plan, compiling and writing a comprehensive history of China from its prehistoric beginnings to the end of the reign of Wu Di in 87 BCE. *The Records of the Grand Historian* is a complex work, including not only a chronological account of events but also biographies of famous figures of the past, histories of important families, and essays on various aspects of Chinese life ranging from the calendar to canals, while simultaneously arguing that Wu Di and his Han predecessors were part of a continuous line of rulers of China that reached back to the very beginnings of its history.

Sima Qian's great work was the model for the series of twenty-four dynastic histories extending from antiquity to the seventeenth century that have made China the most thoroughly documented of all archaic empires. *The Records of the Grand Historian* is more than a history of China, however. Like his older Greek contemporary Polybius, Sima Qian wrote a history of the known world. As a result, their works and those of their successors enable modern historians to trace the emergence of a new order in Afro-Eurasia after the collapse of the Hellenistic state system that was anchored by the two empires of Rome in the west and China in the east, two states that between them contained almost a hundred million people, roughly half the world's population at that time.

For the first time there existed connections, tenuous to be sure, between developments in the east and west thanks to the reappearance of the Iranians as major actors in world history after their two-century-long domination by Alexander the Great and his successors. The Iranians share with the Jews the distinction of being one of the only two peoples of the ancient Near East whose cultural traditions survived the crises of the mid-first millennium CE that marked the end of antiquity. The key to the revival of Iranian culture was the emergence of Parthia as the principal successor state of the Seleucid kingdom. By the first century BCE Parthian territory extended from Mesopotamia in the west to the borders of Bactria in the east, essentially covering contemporary Iraq and Iran. Although Parthian culture was oral, Parthia's strategic location made it of concern to both Rome and China.

As the Parthians also viewed themselves as the heirs of their Persian predecessors, they inevitably came into conflict with the Romans, who were expanding into the Near East in the late second and first centuries BCE. Hostilities between the two states lasted for almost half a century, ending only in 20 BCE with an agreement negotiated by representatives of the emperor Augustus and the contemporary Parthian king that recognized Roman suzerainty over Armenia and Parthian acceptance of the Euphrates River as the border between Roman and Parthian territory. Although the agreement was a diplomatic instead of a military triumph as Romans hungry to erase the stigma of past Parthian victories desired, it guaranteed stability in western Asia until the early second century CE. A key factor in the success of the Roman settlement with Parthia, however, was that for the Parthian kings of the late second and first centuries BCE, their main worry was not Rome but the threat from Shaka nomads seeking to find new homes in Parthian Iran after being pushed out of Bactria by the Yuezhi, who were themselves fleeing the westward expansion of the Xiongnu.

Frontier wars were not, however, the whole of Parthian history. Parthia was a prosperous kingdom filled with towns that had grown wealthy by serving as the principal intermediary in the silk trade between western Asia and the Mediterranean and China, a trade that grew steadily from the second century BCE. The expansion of the silk trade was fueled in the east by diplomatic gifts of Chinese silk to the Xiongnu and other nomad states and in the west by the seemingly insatiable demand of the Roman elite for silk fabrics of all types. Caravans from Parthia are reported to have reached China as early as 106 BCE. The importance of the silk trade to the Parthians is revealed by the first-century CE Chinese historian Ban Gu, who continued Sima Qian's history of the Han Dynasty and not only recorded the arrival at the Han court of Parthian embassies during the first century CE but also told how in 97 CE the Parthians frustrated a Chinese embassy to Rome in order to preserve their monopoly of the silk trade to the west.[2]

Although the Parthian royal residence was located at Ctesiphon, southeast of modern Baghdad, the establishment of the Euphrates River as the border between Roman and Parthian territory meant that Iran was the heart of the kingdom instead of Syria and Mesopotamia, where the Greek legacy was strong. The strengthening of the Iranian character of the Parthian kingdom that had begun in the second century BCE, therefore, continued in the next three centuries. Nevertheless, the decline of Greek culture in Parthia was gradual. It was still possible, for example, in 53 BCE for the head of the defeated Roman general Crassus to be used by a Greek actor as a prop in a performance at the Parthian royal court of Euripides's tragedy the *Bacchae*. By the first century CE, however, the situation had changed. Greek had been replaced in the legends on Parthian coins and in government documents by Iranian, which was written in a new script called Pahlavi; this script had been developed from the Aramaic script that had been used by the Achaemenid administration centuries earlier. Likewise, while the oral nature of Parthian culture limits our knowledge of Parthian religion, indirect evidence—the Avestan character of the names of the Parthian kings and use of the Pahlavi script for Zoroastrian texts—suggests that Zoroastrianism was the dominant religion in Parthian Iran.

The existence of Parthia also changed the course of Roman imperialism. In a passage of the *Aeneid*, the Roman national epic, the late first-century BCE poet Virgil[3] wrote that the sky god Jupiter had granted Rome *imperium sine fine*, "empire without limit," while other Roman poets talked glibly of Rome following the example of Alexander and soon conquering India. For much of the late second and first centuries BCE such dreams did not seem impossible.

Between the death of King Attalus III of Pergamum in 133 BCE and the suicide of Cleopatra VII of Egypt in 30 BCE the whole eastern Mediterranean basin from Anatolia to Egypt came under Roman control. The process was not peaceful. Numerous wars, including three in the early first century BCE with Mithridates VI, the dynamic king of the north Anatolian kingdom of Pontus, and almost two decades of bitter civil war between Roman warlords in the 40s and 30s BCE, were required before the eastern Mediterranean became a Roman lake. Dreams of further expansion in the east ended in the late 20s BCE, however, with Roman acceptance of the independence of Parthia and the almost simultaneous failure of Roman attempts to expand into southern Arabia, Kush, and the central Sahara. Henceforth the focus of Roman imperial dreams would be in central and western Europe.

Until the mid-first century BCE Rome ruled a Mediterranean empire with little interest in expansion into continental Europe. Indeed, it was not until 19 BCE that the Romans gained control of the passes over the Alps and secured access to the principal routes from Italy to central Europe. It is not surprising, therefore, that the first major Roman incursion into the European interior was almost accidental.

Seeking military power and glory to match his rivals Pompey and Crassus, Julius Caesar took advantage of an opportune appeal for help from a Gallic tribe allied to Rome to launch a brutal campaign of conquest in Gaul, essentially modern France, that lasted from 59 BCE to 51 BCE. By the end of the decade all of Gaul from the Mediterranean to the Rhine River had come under Roman rule, albeit at the estimated cost of over a million Gauls killed or enslaved. Resuming Caesar's expansionist policy four decades later, his adopted son and successor, the emperor Augustus, pushed Roman power forward on a broad front from the Black Sea to the North Sea during a two-decade period beginning in 12 BCE. For a brief moment, Rome's frontiers rested on the Danube River in central and southeast Europe and the Elbe River in the northwest until the loss of three whole legions in a German uprising in 9 CE at the Battle of the Teutoburg Forest—the worst Roman defeat in almost two centuries—forced Augustus to recognize the limits of Roman power and withdraw Rome's frontier again to the Rhine River, where it would remain for the next four centuries.

Roman expansion into continental Europe led to massive changes in the culture of prehistoric Europe that were comparable in scope to those caused by the European conquest of the Americas. By the mid-first century BCE agricultural populations sharing similar material culture, primarily Celtic-speaking west of the Rhine River and German-speaking east of it, inhabited much of modern France and Germany. While the Germanic portion of this enormous territory was populated by numerous small farming villages, the rich agricultural potential of Gaul had resulted in a large population and the development of incipient urbanization marked by the spread throughout Gaul of town-sized fortified hilltop settlements that archaeologists call *oppida*.

Julius Caesar's vivid commentaries on his Gallic wars reveal that the *oppida* were ruled by aristocratic oligarchies with the aid of hereditary priests called Druids. Archaeological evidence also indicates that the *oppida* were manufacturing centers and hubs of trade networks that connected the Mediterranean to Britain in the west and central Europe in the east. Moreover, discoveries of coins issued by the *oppida* that were ultimately based on fourth-century BCE Macedonian models suggest that the Gallic economy had begun to be monetized. Likewise, Celtic inscriptions written using the Greek alphabet and references in

The Gundestrup Cauldron is a silver vessel discovered in a peat bog in Denmark. This panel depicts aristocratic cavalry and infantry marching to war to the sound of horns while a large figure at left—probably a god—sacrifices a human victim by drowning. The combination of aristocratic Celtic themes with silver-working technology typical of Thracian workmanship from the Balkans is evidence of the widespread contact between European cultures in the first millennium BCE. Getty Images/Universal Images Group 152206238

classical works to administrative texts indicate that the Gauls also had begun to develop a literate culture.

Establishment of the Rhine as the border between Roman Gaul and free Germany fundamentally altered this situation. The continuity of material culture from Gaul to Germany disappeared. Instead, there is historical and archaeological evidence, particularly the appearance in elite graves and sacrificial deposits of weapons and Roman luxury goods—probably gifts given to favored chieftains by Roman diplomats—that points to the emergence of numerous militarized chiefdoms and a culture of endemic warfare throughout free Germany that fulfilled the early second-century CE Roman historian Tacitus's prayer that "long may the barbarians continue . . . , if not to love us, at least to hate one another."[4]

West of the Rhine in Gaul, meanwhile, the civilization of the *oppida* disappeared. The hilltop settlements encountered by Julius Caesar were abandoned, being gradually replaced during the next two centuries by new cities built in Roman style that were governed by Gallic aristocrats willing to collaborate with their new Roman masters while the warrior values of the Gallic aristocracy were redirected into service in the Roman military. The consolidation of Roman rule was a long process, of course, lasting more than a century and punctuated by repeated rebellions during which the Druids, whose prophecies of Gallic freedom and cultural renewal inspired resistance to Rome, were suppressed together with their cults. Gallic culture was essentially decapitated, resulting in the emergence in the new cities of Gaul of a hybrid culture, increasingly Roman in organization and Latin in language among the urban elite, while its pre-Roman language and religious traditions primarily survived at the level of folk culture among the rural population.

The dramatic expansion of Rome's empire in the late second and the early first centuries BCE was paralleled by the almost simultaneous and equally dramatic collapse of the Roman Republic and the return of monarchy to Rome after five centuries of absence. However, it was not a revolution in the usual sense of the term that brought down the Republic but a series of interlocking crises that lasted from the late 130s BCE to the end of the 30s BCE. The crises began with the unsuccessful attempts of the Gracchi brothers to restore the central position of small farmers in Roman life and their tragic deaths in the late 130s and 120s BCE, and they ended with the failed dictatorship of Julius Caesar and the civil wars of the late 40s and 30s BCE that determined which of his successors would rule Rome. At one point in early 80 BCE, Rome's existence itself was even threatened by a brutal war against its Italian allies that ended, however, with the extension of Roman citizenship to all inhabitants of Italy, a critical step in the social and cultural unification of the Italian peninsula.

No single cause explains these disparate events, but underlying all of them was one fundamental reality. Rome's political institutions, which had developed in the early Republic to govern a small city-state, were inadequate to manage a continent-wide empire and to control the Roman army and its commanders, on whom the security of the empire depended. As a result, the Senate, whose influence had grown during the third and second centuries BCE, steadily lost power during the last century of the republic to a series of warlords, men whose power ultimately rested on the personal loyalty of the armies they commanded: Marius, Sulla, Pompey, Julius Caesar, and the last and greatest of them all, Julius Caesar's adopted son, Gaius Octavius, the later emperor Augustus, to name only the most prominent.

Building a new Roman monarchy took the whole of Augustus's long reign from 30 BCE to 14 CE. The process was difficult, although he had some important advantages. The most fundamental was that like Qin Shihuangdi, Augustus benefited from the Romans' exhaustion from decades of civil war and political strife. Those conflicts also had decimated the Senate, eliminating the bitterest opponents of his new order. Finally, the integration into the Roman upper class of the Italian elite, who had received Roman citizenship early in the first century BCE, provided him with a reservoir of reliable supporters for his reforms.

The system that Augustus built rested on transformation of the Roman army into a salaried professional force loyal to Augustus that was financed by the revenues generated by the tribute of the empire and led by officers appointed by him; creation of the nucleus of an imperial administration staffed by Augustus's personal slaves and freedmen; and reconciliation of the Senate to the new monarchy by concealing it behind the façade of what he called the "restoration of the Republic," the scrupulous maintenance of the fiction that he was not a king but the *Princeps*—the first citizen—or as Augustus[5] described his position in the summary of his achievements he drew up at the end of his life, "I surpassed everyone in influence, but I had no more power than other men who were my colleagues in public office."

Not all of Augustus's initiatives, of course, were equally successful. The disastrous failure of his German policy has already been mentioned. Similarly unsuccessful were the pro-natalist laws he promoted to reverse the shrinking numbers of aristocratic families, only to find himself forced to exile his daughter and granddaughter, both named Julia,

The complex imagery of the marble statue known as Augustus of Prima Porta *epitomizes Roman imperial ideology. The figure of Eros on a dolphin next to his right leg alludes to Augustus's legendary descent from the goddess Venus, while the depiction of the Parthian king on his armor celebrates Augustus's diplomatic victory over Parthia.* Erich Lessing/Art Resource, NY ART29576

in accordance with the penalties prescribed by his own laws on adultery. Nevertheless, most of his initiatives were more successful. Most obvious were the enormous building programs that finally began the transformation of Rome into a capital appropriate to the empire it ruled. Other initiatives provided the city for the first time with rudimentary fire and police agencies and expanded the welfare programs for its citizens that had begun a century earlier with Gaius Gracchus's law authorizing the sale of grain at subsidized low prices during food shortages.

Augustus's most important achievement, however, was that when he died in 14 CE his system had become the new establishment. As the historian Tacitus despairingly asked, "How many people had seen the Republic?"[6] With the majority of the Senate and other members of the Roman elite owing their positions to the Augustan system, its survival was assured despite its flaws, not the least of which was the lack of a mechanism for choosing a successor to Augustus. The proof lies in a simple fact. In spite of all the eccentricities of his four successors—Tiberius, Caligula, Claudius, and Nero—whose crimes fill the pages of Roman historians, no one questioned that there would be an emperor. Even when rebellious Roman armies created four emperors in two years during the crisis of the years 68 to 70 CE, these events did not lead to a movement to restore the republic but to the establishment of a new dynasty, the Flavian, which ruled the Roman Empire until 96 CE. Not for another century would Rome face another succession crisis comparable to the year of the four emperors, and that crisis would also end in the establishment of a new dynasty, that of the Severi, who would rule the empire until 235 CE.

These two centuries also saw major changes in Roman society, albeit not in the lives of the vast majority of Romans, whose existence continued to revolve around marriage, family, and the struggle to earn a living. The same was true even for the handful of elite women who benefited from Augustus's law that women who bore three children were freed from the obligation to have a male guardian and could therefore manage their own property. The composition of Roman society itself, however, changed dramatically.

Most far-reaching was the cultural unification of Italy, thanks to the extension of Roman citizenship to all Italians in the wake of the Social War. As a result, the Latin language and Roman identity spread throughout the peninsula, gradually replacing ancient local languages and cultures such as Etruscan. Almost equally far-reaching was the transformation of Rome itself. The city was a powerful magnet, which drew migrants—both slave and free—from all over the empire, attracted

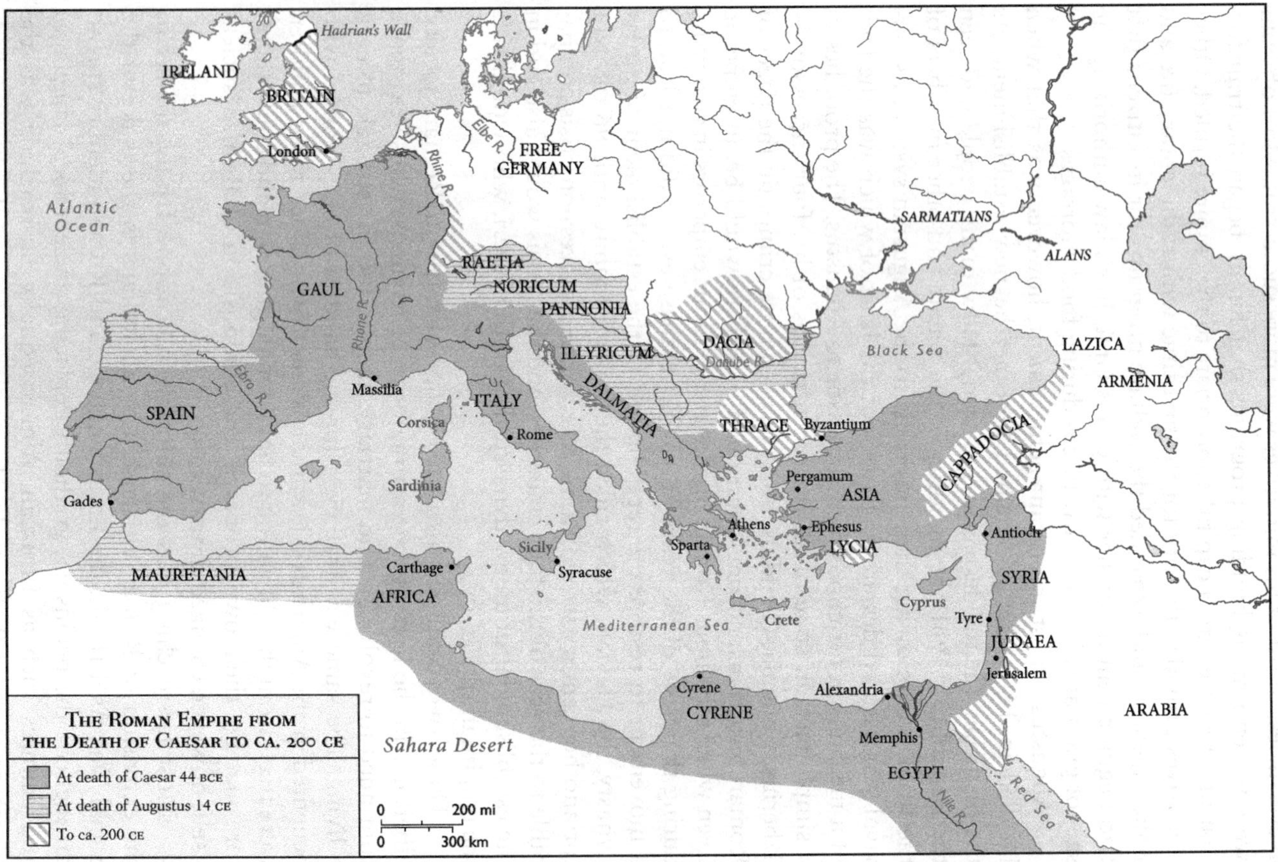
Hadrian's Wall
IRELAND
BRITAIN
London
Atlantic Ocean
Elbe R.
Rhine R.
FREE GERMANY
SARMATIANS
ALANS
RAETIA
NORICUM
PANNONIA
GAUL
Rhone R.
Ebro R.
SPAIN
Gades
Massilia
Corsica
Sardinia
ITALY
Rome
ILLYRICUM
DALMATIA
DACIA
Danube R.
Black Sea
LAZICA
ARMENIA
THRACE
Byzantium
CAPPADOCIA
Pergamum
ASIA
Athens
Ephesus
Sparta
LYCIA
Antioch
Sicily
Syracuse
Carthage
AFRICA
MAURETANIA
SYRIA
Cyprus
Crete
Mediterranean Sea
Tyre
JUDAEA
Jerusalem
Cyrene
CYRENE
Alexandria
Memphis
EGYPT
Nile R.
Red Sea
ARABIA
Sahara Desert
0 200 mi
0 300 km
The Roman Empire from the Death of Caesar to ca. 200 CE
At death of Caesar 44 BCE
At death of Augustus 14 CE
To ca. 200 CE

by the wealth flowing into the capital. By the end of the first century CE Rome had become a multiethnic city with large communities of Greeks, Jews, and Egyptians, to name only the most prominent. Today, all that remains of these communities are their epitaphs and the catacombs where they buried many of their dead and prejudicial comments in Latin literature, such as the early second-century CE satirist Juvenal's furious beginning of his satiric description of life in Rome: "I can't bear a Greek Rome."[7] In antiquity, however, these communities were the centers of vibrant diasporas (dispersion of a people from their homeland) that were the principal conduits for the introduction into Rome of new religions such as Judaism, Christianity, and the Egyptian cult of Isis and Osiris.

The first century BCE was also the classical period of Roman literature. The authors whose works were standard textbooks in European education for almost two millennia all wrote during this period, men like the orator and politician Cicero, the historians Julius Caesar and Livy, and the poets Horace, Ovid, and Virgil. The development of this

Panel from the Arch of Titus depicting the entry into Rome of the menorah and other furnishings of the temple in Jerusalem, which was looted and burned at the end of the Jewish rebellion in 70 CE. The destruction of the temple marked the end of Judaism as a temple-centered and priest-led religion and the beginning of rabbinic Judaism, which became the dominant form of the religion. Photo by Stanley Burstein

literature was dominated by three themes, which were the standardization of Latin as a literary language, the deliberate creation in Latin of a classical literature that would rival Greek literature, and the celebration of the achievements of Rome. In the process much of the content of Greek thought was incorporated in the new Latin literature, facilitating its transfer and preservation in the increasingly Latin-speaking elite culture of southern and western Europe. Equally important, the literature of the late Republic and early Roman Empire also reflected the multi-ethnic character of first-century BCE Rome. With few exceptions such as Julius Caesar, the principal authors of this period were not Romans but citizens of Italian cities who had received Roman citizenship after the Social War or assimilated provincials like the Gaul Pompeius Trogus, who wrote in Latin an influential history of the peoples conquered by Rome, and pro-Roman Greeks such as the rhetorician Dionysius of Halicarnassus, who argued in his history of the early Republic that Rome was really a Greek city, and the geographer Strabo, who compiled a monumental geography of the known world that emphasized Rome's civilizing mission.

It was not only the Roman West that was affected by the emergence of Parthia as a significant Eurasian power. Its effects were felt also in central and south Asia. Parthia's successful defense against nomad invasions into Iran and subsequent expansion toward Bactria deflected first the Shaka and then the Yuezhi south into northwest India. The India they entered was divided into a multitude of competing kingdoms of which the most important were those of the Shungas in the Ganges Valley and the Satavahanas in the Deccan. The invasions of the Shakas and Yuezhi therefore complicated an already complex political situation.

Far-reaching changes occurred as a result in India, two of which were particularly noteworthy. First, by the end of the first century BCE, the last of the Indo-Greek kingdoms had disappeared, eliminating what remained of Alexander's conquests in Bactria and India. Second, Kujula Kadphises, the leader of the Kuei-shuang tribe of the Yuezhi, united the five tribes of the Yuezhi, founding a kingdom that extended from Bactria into northwest India and formed the nucleus of the Kushan Empire that by the early second century CE included the whole region from the Oxus River in the north to the Ganges Valley in the south, connecting in the process Parthia in the west and China in the east to India in the south.

Despite its chaotic politics in which kingdoms' power and territories expanded and contracted like an accordion, India was generally prosperous, marked by the growth of trade. The activity of Indian traders extended at least from the Red Sea port of Berenike in Egypt in the west to southeast Asia in the east and Sri Lanka in the south to central Asia in the north. And they prospered. In an autobiographical inscription composed in elegant Greek that was set up by a main road in Bactria, a Greek-educated Indian merchant named Sophytos, son of Naratos,[8] tells how after his family lost all its wealth he "left home ... and went to many cities and blamelessly gained great wealth." Indian literary works such as the collection of moralizing stories called the *Pañcatantra* also celebrate the wealth to be gained by trade in foreign lands:

> In life, those expert in buying and selling
> who travel to distant lands for trading
> double and triple their fortunes
> through their unflagging exertions.[9]

Vivid evidence of the wealth of such merchants survives in the numerous donations they made to Buddhist and Jain monasteries and to the construction of Buddhist stupas and massive dining halls excavated into the sides of mountains in the Deccan.

Prosperity also was accompanied by the growth of cities, some ancient like the intellectual center of Taxila and some new like the Kushan capital of Mathura. New wealth, expanded cities, and the proliferation of kingdoms ruled by foreign dynasties inevitably also impacted social life. The cities, for example, were the home of the sophisticated society described in the *Kama Sutra*. At the same time, the growth of cities and the opportunities that were found in them also threatened to undermine the Varna system so that in *The Laws of Manu* Brahmins and members of the other three highest Varnas are allowed to follow occupations normally forbidden to them, without incurring impurity, in case of economic need. So, for example, "a priest who cannot make a living by his own innate activity may make his living by fulfilling the duty of a ruler" or "he may make his living by farming and tending livestock, the livelihood of a commoner."[10]

Fundamental cultural changes also occurred during the period. Alongside the sacrifices that formed the heart of traditional Indian worship, new cults appeared devoted to the personal worship of individual deities, particularly Vishnu, the creator of cosmic order, and Shiva, the destroyer. The newly rich merchants and the foreign princes, however, directed their patronage toward Jainism and especially Buddhism, which were not so tightly intertwined with the Varna system. Particularly attractive to them was the Mahayana form of Buddhism with its emphasis on the possibility that anyone could become a Buddha and its reverence for Bodhisattvas, individuals of supreme moral worth who freely

The Kushan Empire of Kanishka I (around 129–152 CE) had a cosmopolitan culture combining central Asian, Indian, and Greek elements. This rare coin depicts a bearded Kanishka leaning on a sword and wearing a typical nomadic costume of trousers and robe. On the reverse is an image of Buddha with his name spelled out in Greek letters. Private collection CNG, Inc.

delayed their attainment of nirvana to assist humanity to reach similar perfection. Codified in a rich and diverse Sanskrit literature and patronized by the Kushan emperors, particularly Kanishka the Great, Mahayana Buddhism spread together with Indian merchants along trade routes throughout central Asia, ultimately reaching China in the second century CE.

Literature and art also flourished. The rich corpus of Mahayana Buddhist works composed during this period has already been mentioned. In addition, internal evidence indicates that a wide range of classical Sanskrit texts including *The Laws of Manu*, *Arthashastra*, and *Ramayana* also had reached their final form by the first century CE, while royal inscriptions point to the existence of a now lost body of literature celebrating the achievements of kings. In the Gandhara region of northwest India, moreover, sculptors familiar with styles and techniques of Hellenistic Greek sculpture created the first figural Buddhist art, modeling representations of the Buddha on images of Apollo and even including themes from the Trojan War in the decoration of Buddhist stupas. Greek influence was not limited to art but extended to astronomy and astrology as evidenced by the existence of Sanskrit translations of Greek astronomical texts and the adoption of the zodiac by Indian astronomers.

The ultimate origin of much of the political upheaval in central and south Asia, however, lay farther east in China, specifically in the failure

Second-century CE relief, which probably formed part of a Buddhist monument in the Gandhara region of northwest India. The scene shows the priest Laocoön probing the Trojan horse while the princess Cassandra (far left) predicts the fall of Troy. The depiction of a scene from a Greek epic on a Buddhist monument in a mixture of Classical and Indian styles reflects the integration of Greek and Indian cultures in the Hellenistic period. © The Trustees of the British Museum 00100175001

of the *heqin* or "Peace and Kinship" policy adopted by Liu Bang in the early second century BCE. Many Chinese political figures and intellectuals always had found the *heqin* policy both humiliating and expensive: 200,000 liters of wine, 92,400 meters of silk, and 1,000 ounces of gold in annual tribute.[11] The humiliation and the extortionate cost would have been bearable, however, if it had achieved its primary goal, peace on China's northern frontier, but that it signally failed to do.

During the approximately half century of their existence, renewals of the *heqin* agreements were repeatedly followed by nomad raids into Chinese territory and demands for increased payments and the opening of markets where the Xiongnu could trade. The root of the problem, of course, was the *shanyu*'s need, on the one hand, for Chinese luxuries to reward his followers and his inability, on the other hand, to fulfill his obligations under the *heqin* system by preventing Xiongnu chieftains from conducting independent raids. Be that as it may, the Han emperors had used the relative peace bought by the *heqin* policy to rebuild China's military strength, allowing Sima Qian's master Wu Di to go on the offensive in central Asia with the intention of destroying the Xiongnu Empire.

For almost two decades, beginning in the 130s BCE, Chinese forces, often numbering in the tens of thousands of men, campaigned in central Asia. The results were dramatic as Wu Di's forces not only retook the Ordos region, but they also extended Han power throughout the Tarim basin and drove the Xiongnu north of the Gobi Desert. Henceforth Wu Di and his successors would offer peace to the Xiongnu only on condition that the *shanyu* provide a hostage, send tribute, and pay homage to China. It took almost a further three quarters of a century of conflict and a civil war between factions of the Xiongnu before the *shanyu* of the southern Xiongnu agreed to the Chinese terms in 54 BCE, not least because he realized that in practice the new system did not significantly differ from the old *heqin* system since the Chinese government would provide the Xiongnu with rich gifts and opportunities for trade in exchange for tribute that was more symbolic than substantive.

The submission of the southern Xiongnu in 54 BCE did, however, mark the end of the Xiongnu Empire as the dominant power in central Asia, but the Chinese victory came at a high price. The costs of the constant military campaigning in central Asia and controlling the territories won by it brought the Han state close to bankruptcy, which was averted only by burdensome taxation paid mostly by the peasantry and the establishment of government monopolies of key areas of the economy, including such essentials as iron and salt. As was the case in Rome, frontier wars also fundamentally changed the nature of the Chinese army. Because infantry was ineffective in central Asia, Wu Di's successors gradually phased out universal military service, relying instead on elite cavalry forces composed mainly of nomad mercenaries and supported by elite forces of crossbowmen and garrison troops consisting of short-term levies and convicts.

The effects of the collapse of the Xiongnu Empire were felt throughout north China. As China's northern frontier became unstable, weak nomad tribes fleeing their more powerful neighbors sought protection by seeking permission to settle in Chinese territory. The result was much the same as would be the case when the Roman Empire implemented similar policies in late antiquity. From the Han government's perspective, manpower to populate the frontier regions made the nomad requests attractive, but the reality was that the Chinese government lost control of much of its northern frontier as large swathes of territory were surrendered to tribal groups that were linked to the Chinese government only by their chiefs, whose doubtful loyalty was concealed by their appointments as Chinese officials.

The Xiongnu wars also fundamentally changed Chinese society. For the peasantry, the end of universal military service cut off the possibility of upward mobility through success in battle that had been made possible by the Qin rank system. The result in an overwhelmingly agrarian society like China was the hardening of the divide between the peasantry, who paid the heavy taxes and provided the labor service required by the Han system, and the landed rich, who dominated local government. At the same time, recruitment into government service was increasingly restricted to graduates of the imperial university, which had thirty thousand students by the beginning of the second century CE. While the bureaucracy grew to more than one hundred thousand officials, politics centered increasingly on conflict between factions trying to control the series of child emperors who succeeded Wu Di. The ambitious attempt by a regent named Wang Mang failed; he had seized power in 9 CE and sought to solve China's problems by reforms based on an idealized idea of the organization of society in the Zhou period including land redistribution and the abolition of slavery. His reign lasted only seventeen years and ended in revolution and the restoration of the Han Dynasty in 23 CE with the support of the newly empowered landed aristocracy. While the restored Han Dynasty held the throne for another two centuries until the abdication of the last Han emperor in 220 CE, none of the regime's fundamental problems had been solved so that its later history continued to revolve around conflicts over the control of minor emperors between the palace eunuchs and the families of the emperors' consorts.

Despite the political turbulence during the Han Dynasty, art and literature flourished, particularly history, which reached its classic form in the work of the first-century CE historian Ban Gu. Ban Gu belonged to a literary family, and like his great predecessor and model Sima Qian, Ban Gu undertook to complete a work begun by his father. In Ban Gu's case, however, his history had to be finished after his death in prison in 92 CE by his sister Ban Zhao, who was an imperial official and a distinguished scholar and advocate for women's education, as well as the author of a manual of appropriate female behavior entitled *Lessons for Women* that characterized the ideal woman as one who "modestly yield(s) to others; let her respect others; let her put others first, herself last."[12] Also, unlike *The Records of the Grand Historian*, The *History of the Western Han Dynasty* was an official history that was based on archival sources made available to Ban Gu by Emperor Ming and to his sister by Emperor He; it argued that the legitimacy of

According to Chinese religious belief, after death a person continued to enjoy the same social position and privileges he or she had during life. By the Han period, aristocratic tombs contained numerous statuettes of servants and models of buildings, such as this multi-story tower house, called mingqi *(spirit articles) that were intended to replicate the social world familiar to the dead person during his or her life.* Nelson-Atkins Museum of Art, Kansas City

the Han Dynasty was based on the transfer of the mandate of heaven to it from the Qin Dynasty.

Royal patronage was not limited to historiography but extended to other areas of Han intellectual life. It was the early Han emperors' appointment of professors for each of the five Confucian classics at the imperial academy and their support for the scholars' efforts to determine reliable texts for those works that made Confucianism central to the training of government officials and determined the direction of Confucian scholarship for centuries. Predictably, the only challenge to the dominance of Confucianism came from an emperor, the mid-second-century emperor Huan, who sought support from Daoists. They had formed a virtual church devoted to the worship of the deified Laozi, the legendary founder of Daoism, until the outbreak of the Daoist-led Yellow Turban Revolt in 184 CE ended royal patronage of Daoism. In view of the examples of historiography and philosophy, it is not surprising that henceforth the emperor was the assumed audience for the works of elite Chinese authors, no matter the subject.

In a passage of his *Annals*, his history of the first four Roman emperors, the historian Tacitus lamented that, unlike his Republican predecessors, he could only write about things of trifling importance, "peace wholly unbroken or but slightly disturbed, dismal misery in the capital, an emperor careless about the enlargement of the empire."[13] At the other end of Eurasia his older contemporary, the Chinese historian Ban Gu, could have said much the same thing. In both empires politics consisted of little more than the bitter feuds of court factions, and geographical and logistical difficulties had put an end to dreams of imperial expansion. The result was that four empires—Roman, Parthian, Kushan, and Han Chinese—whose dynasties claimed divine authority for their rule dominated temperate Afro-Eurasia from the Atlantic to the Pacific.

Historians like Tacitus might complain about the lack of military glory in their time, but for the populations of these empires, their coexistence ensured an unprecedented degree of stability and even prosperity for some, albeit not for all as the outbreak of peasant revolts like the Yellow Turban in China and widespread banditry in the Roman Empire reveal. Still, the stability was real, and it made possible increasing trade and cultural exchange throughout Afro-Eurasia. Society also became more complex as the new capital cities grew and attracted immigrants, becoming home to multiethnic diasporas. The period also was one of great cultural creativity. Royal patronage fostered the growth of classical literatures that would form the basis of elite education and artistic and architectural forms that would provide visual expressions of imperial ideology as long as the empires survived.

CHAPTER 7

Crisis and Recovery

(Third Century CE*)*

Sometime in 203 CE or 204 CE an anonymous Christian author published a remarkable work, the diary of a young Roman woman and mother named Vibia Perpetua, who was executed together with five companions in the amphitheater at Carthage. Perpetua's diary, one of the few surviving works of Latin literature written by an educated woman, suggests that her family belonged to the ruling elite of Roman Carthage. What brought her to a humiliating death in the amphitheater, a fate members of her class were normally spared, was her public declaration to the Proconsul—governor—of Africa that "I am a Christian" in defiance of an edict of the Roman emperor Septimius Severus forbidding conversion to Judaism or Christianity. Her death was not easy. Perpetua vividly recounted in her diary dreams she had in prison in which she defeated predominantly male demons seeking to dissuade her from seeking martyrdom, the humiliations she endured from her guards, her rejection of the pleas of her father to recant her confession, and her cutting the final tie to her family by surrendering her baby to her parents. The book closes with an eyewitness account of her death in the arena at the hands of a gladiator after she survived being tossed by a wild cow.[1]

That Christians, particularly those from elite families such as Vibia Perpetua, would willingly face horrible deaths in the name of an obscure Jewish preacher executed for sedition during the reign of the emperor Tiberius baffled Romans such as the second-century CE Stoic philosopher-emperor Marcus Aurelius; he agreed that a person should be ready to die "but that readiness should be the result of personal judgment and not simple obstinacy as is the case with Christians."[2] Their confusion was understandable. Christianity was something unprecedented in Roman experience, an underground religious movement with organized communities of believers that had spread not only throughout

A wall painting from Pompeii that probably dates from the first century CE. *The image is thought to be an idealized portrait of the Greek poetess Sappho, who is represented as an educated Roman woman, holding a stylus in her left hand and in her right hand a codex—several wooden strips covered in wax tied together to form a notebook—in which she could write drafts of her poems.* Scala/Art Resource, NY ART7541

the empire but also far beyond its borders into the kingdom of Parthia and even to western India.

Christianity was not the only religion to expand dramatically during this period. Three quarters of a century after Perpetua's death a remarkable religious teacher named Mani died in a Persian prison. Born into a Judaizing sect in Mesopotamia, Mani had traveled widely in Iran and western India before proclaiming himself the successor of the Buddha and Jesus and the founder of a religion that mingled ideas from Christianity, Zoroastrianism, Hinduism, and Buddhism. At his death, his followers, known as Manichaeans, could be found throughout Iran and Mesopotamia and even in the Roman Empire. Still farther east Mahayana Buddhism enjoyed similar success, spreading from its home in northern India throughout the central Asian territories of the Kushan Empire and finally reaching China in the second century CE.

The remarkable spread of new religions was just one example of the dynamism of life in the second century CE, a period that the great eighteenth-century CE English historian of the Roman Empire Edward Gibbon characterized as "the period in the history of the world, during which the condition of the human race was most happy and prosperous,"[3] at least, that is, for members of the social and economic elite like Perpetua and her family. Evidence of the prosperity people like Perpetua took for granted is found throughout Afro-Eurasia in the ruins of ancient cities and religious and military structures still visited by tourists. Underlying this prosperity was a dramatic increase in connectivity throughout Afro-Eurasia that made this period the first truly global era in world history. As in later periods of globalization, far-reaching social and economic changes accompanied the growth in connectivity. Although such changes occurred from one end of Afro-Eurasia to the other, they are most fully documented in Gaul at the western extremity of the Roman Empire.

A little over a century and a quarter before Perpetua met her death in the arena at Carthage, the Gauls made one last attempt to break free of Roman rule. Only in 70 CE after two years of bitter fighting throughout northern Gaul and the Rhine valley did Roman forces succeed in suppressing the rebellion. Suppression of the great Gallic rebellion was followed by dramatic changes in Gaul in the next century, changes that are paralleled elsewhere in the western provinces of the Roman Empire.

In the interior of Gaul, Roman-style cities appeared at strategic points on the rivers, and proliferating in the countryside were large farms centered on rich farmhouses decorated with elegant mosaics and classical statues that archaeologists call villas. The driving force behind the urbanization of Gaul was the Roman desire to limit the growth of bureaucracy by delegating responsibility for local government to local elites who were encouraged to "build temples, market-places, and town houses" in the words of the historian Tacitus,[4] himself a Roman senator from Gaul and proof of the success of the policy. Equally important were the changes in Gallic intellectual culture. So, while elements of Gallic religion survived into late antiquity, elite culture became Romanized following the suppression of the Druids and the introduction of Roman education. As a result, by the fourth century CE among the leading intellectuals in the Roman Empire were Romanized Gallic aristocrats, some of whom even claimed descent from Druidic families.

At the same time, the frontier between Gaul and free Germany was hardened. Throughout the Rhine valley monumental stone forts were built to house the forty thousand men of the eight legions that guarded the frontier. The shanty towns surrounding the forts that had once housed bars and brothels gradually grew into regular towns; these became home to legionary veterans and the families they formed with their native wives, and grew to be important future cites such as Mainz, Cologne, and Trier, from which Latin culture spread in northern Gaul. In addition to the major legionary forts, a complex network of roads, ditches, minor forts, and palisades that archaeologists call the *limes* stretched along the frontier from the sea to far into the interior.

At first glance, the system seemed perfectly designed to serve as a formidable barrier separating Roman territory from the barbarian world beyond, but looks are deceiving. Like the Chinese walls at the other end of Afro-Eurasia, the purpose of the *limes* was not to divide Romans and barbarians but to regulate contact between them, contact that, as in China, was driven by the needs of the army that guarded the frontier. Roman legions consumed vast amounts of supplies of all kinds; archaeologists found a million iron nails in an abandoned British fort. Huge amounts of foodstuffs, metal goods, and animals and animal products, especially leather, flowed into the forts not only from Gaul, where supplying the army sparked economic growth, but also from across the border in free Germany, where archaeologists have discovered the remains of farms and cattle ranches that supplied the legions. Numerous finds of imported Roman goods, coins, and weapons in graves and sacrificial deposits attest to the spread of Roman material culture and, more ominously, knowledge of Roman military tactics into free Germany as a result.

Economic expansion during the second century CE was not limited to Gaul but involved the whole Roman Empire. An empire-wide trade in commodities including wine, grain, building stone, metals, and slaves was required to support megacities like Rome and Alexandria. A remarkable archaeological site at Rome reveals the vast scale of this trade: Monte Testaccio. Monte Testaccio is an artificial hill composed of tens of millions of broken amphorae—ceramic storage vessels capable of holding seventy liters of liquid—that were used to transport olive oil from southern Spain to Rome during the first two and a half centuries CE. Two centuries of prosperity fueled by an improving climate—the Roman warm period—set the stage for an unprecedented expansion of trade throughout Afro-Eurasia.

The varied evidence, which includes allusions in Greek, Latin, Indian, and Chinese literature and numerous archaeological discoveries scattered from the Atlantic to the Pacific, points to a level of international trade not reached again until the late Middle Ages. In central Asia the extension of Han authority into the Tarim Basin and the consolidation of the Kushan Empire provided security for caravans moving along routes that historians call the Silk Roads. While little is known about the early history of the Silk Roads, the so-called Begram treasure discovered in Afghanistan—possibly the contents of a royal Kushan storehouse—with its combination of Roman glass and bronze wares, Indian ivories, and Chinese lacquer works reveals the varied sources of the goods carried by the Silk Road caravans. Great wealth was to be made in the caravan trade between the east and the west, but individuals like a Roman merchant named Maes Titianus, whose agents traveled the whole route from the Mediterranean to China were rare. Instead, the profits fell to the middlemen, who controlled the stages along the routes traversed by the caravans: Sogdians in central Asia, Parthians, and Palmyrenes in Syria.

While the Silk Road trade has attracted most popular attention, larger in scale was the maritime trading network that connected Egypt and the Mediterranean basin to east Africa, Arabia, and south Asia via the Red Sea and Indian Ocean. Knowledge of the regularity of the monsoon wind system in the Indian Ocean had reached Egypt in the late Hellenistic period. Combined with the introduction of strongly built ships able to withstand its gale force winds while carrying large cargoes, regular use of the direct sea route from Egypt to India became feasible for the first time.

At the same time, Roman unification of the Mediterranean basin created a strong western market for eastern goods such as Chinese silk, pearls, spices, and especially black pepper from southwest India, which quickly became a staple of Roman cuisine. Meanwhile in south Asia, Buddhists increasingly used Chinese silk for banners and made dedications consisting of the so-called seven jewels—gold, silver, lapis lazuli, seashell, agate, pearl, and carnelian, some of which were of western origin. The result was the creation of continent-wide demand that propelled the expansion of the Indian Ocean trade.

Historians have long misunderstood the character and extent of this trade, primarily because moralizing Roman writers treated it as a wasteful trade in useless luxuries such as silk whose only purpose, according to the Roman encyclopedist Pliny the Elder, was "to make it possible for a Roman lady to wear transparent clothes in public."[5] As a result, the ancient Asian trade has been viewed as a small-scale, one-sided exchange of oriental exotica such as silks and spices for Roman silver and gold currency. In fact, however, incense and spices were essential to Roman culture and import taxes levied on the trade were a major source of revenue for the Roman government. The reality is revealed by the *Periplus of the Erythraean Sea*, a guide to sailing and trading conditions in the Indian Ocean, written in the mid-first century CE by a Greco-Egyptian merchant, which depicts a very different trade, one in which a wide variety of goods moved in both directions in response to changes in demand. A revealing snapshot of the real character of the trade is provided by the *Periplus*'s description of goods that were imported and exported at Barygaza, modern Bharuch, the most important port in northwest India:

In this port of trade there is a market for wine, principally Italian ... ; copper tin, and lead; coral ... , all kinds of clothing with no adornment or of printed fabric, multicolored girdles, eighteen inches wide; storax; yellow sweet clover; raw glass; realgar; sulphide of antimony; Roman money, gold and silver, which commands an exchange at some profit against the local currency; unguent, inexpensive and in limited quantity. For the king there was imported in those times precious silverware, slave musicians, beautiful girls for concubinage, fine wine, expensive clothing with no adornment, and choice unguent. These are exports: nard, costus, bdellium; ivory; onyx; agate; ... cotton cloth of all kinds; Chinese cloth [i.e., silk]; ... silk yarn; long pepper; and items brought here from the nearby ports of trade.[6]

Globalization also extended the network of contacts among peoples. For example, while Romans believed India was the source of most of the exotic goods they desired, the reality was different. Indian merchants actually served as middlemen for many goods whose actual origins were farther east, seeking silks, for example, in China and spices such as cinnamon, which Romans valued for medicinal purposes, in Indonesia, and incidentally preparing the way for the spread of Indian religion and art into southeast Asia in the late first millennium CE.

A similar process occurred in the west. There the demand for African products such as gold, slaves, and especially wild animals for the Roman games—the emperor Trajan, for example, had eleven thousand beasts slaughtered in 107 CE to celebrate the conquest of Dacia, modern Romania—exterminated most of the *megafauna* of north Africa and forced Romans to extend their search for animals for the arena into the African interior. The result was the beginning of the integration of sub-Saharan Africa into the Afro-Eurasian global network.

Early Greek and Roman accounts of the African interior are a confusing mixture of fact and fiction for understandable reasons. As a result of being isolated for over two millennia from the Mediterranean basin by the drying out of the Sahara, sub-Saharan Africa was a virtual new world to the peoples of the Afro-Eurasian civilizations, almost as strange as the Americas would be to sixteenth-century CE Europeans. As in the case of the Americas, Greek and Roman writers described the inhabitants of the African interior as strange peoples like the headless Blemmyes whose eyes were in their chests and the Strapfeet whose feet were shaped like thongs. In actuality, however, by the early centuries CE, a variety of complex societies ranging from autonomous villages to large states covered much of central and southern Africa, an area larger

The fullest illustration of the exotic animal trade in the Roman Empire is the seventy-meter-long Great Hunt Mosaic in the Piazza Armerina, an elaborate villa in southern Sicily built in the early fourth century CE. *Here, an African elephant is loaded onto a ship while hunters round up a camel and a tiger. These diverse species indicate the wide range of the trade, which extended from north Africa to south Asia.* Erich Lessing/Art Resource, NY ART74858

than western Europe, thanks to one of the great population movements of world history, the Bantu Expansion.

The Bantu Expansion was a gradual process that took several millennia to complete, during which proto-Bantu speakers spread south and east from their home in Cameroon and Nigeria, absorbing along the way foraging and farming populations. In the process, Bantu speakers learned from peoples they encountered in central and east Africa how to farm grain crops and use iron. Population increased, society became more complex, and trade expanded to meet the growing demand for iron and other products, leading to the emergence of trading and manufacturing towns, where goods from different ecological zones could be exchanged and transported by water.

These processes were most intense in west Africa where early states had appeared by the late first millennium BCE. The best known of these early states is the Nok culture in modern Nigeria. The Nok culture is famous for the remarkable terra cotta figures discovered by modern tin miners that probably were intended for dedication in shrines. Their creators were a mystery until archaeological discoveries revealed that the Nok culture was created by iron-using farmers over a period of seven hundred years from around 500 BCE to roughly 200 CE.

Even more remarkable were developments in the inland delta of the Niger River in Mali, where the first cities in sub-Saharan Africa emerged. Early urbanization is best documented at the site of Jenne-Jeno. Founded as a village about 200 BCE in a fertile area watered by the Niger River, Jenne grew until by the late first millennium CE it was a walled city approximately eighty-one acres in extent surrounded by a cluster of villages, each of which seems to have specialized in a particular craft such as iron working. The secret of Jenne's prosperity was its location, which allowed easy access to the salt and mineral resources of the Sahara to the north and to the animal and plant products and eventually the gold of the forest zone to the south, and made it the center of a regional trade network covering much of the Niger basin and its hinterlands.

It was the desire to acquire African goods that led to the end of the isolation of sub-Saharan Africa from the rest of Afro-Eurasia by the first century CE. While Carthaginian efforts to reach sub-Saharan Africa by way of the Atlantic Ocean failed, the millennia-old, seaborne trading networks of the Indian Ocean made contact almost inevitable. Indeed, archaeological evidence for the cultivation of bananas, a fruit native to southeast Asia, in west Africa as early as around 500 BCE suggests that Austronesian speakers from southeast Asia were already visiting east Africa by that time.

Full integration of the east African coast into the Indian Ocean commercial network, however, had to wait for the expansion of trade between the Mediterranean and south Asia in the first and second centuries CE. Already by the mid-first century CE Arab traders were visiting Tanzania under the protection of the kingdom of Himyar in Yemen, intermarrying with local populations and trading with coastal chiefdoms manufactured metal goods of all kinds, wine, grain for ivory, rhinoceros horn, high-quality tortoise shell, and slaves.

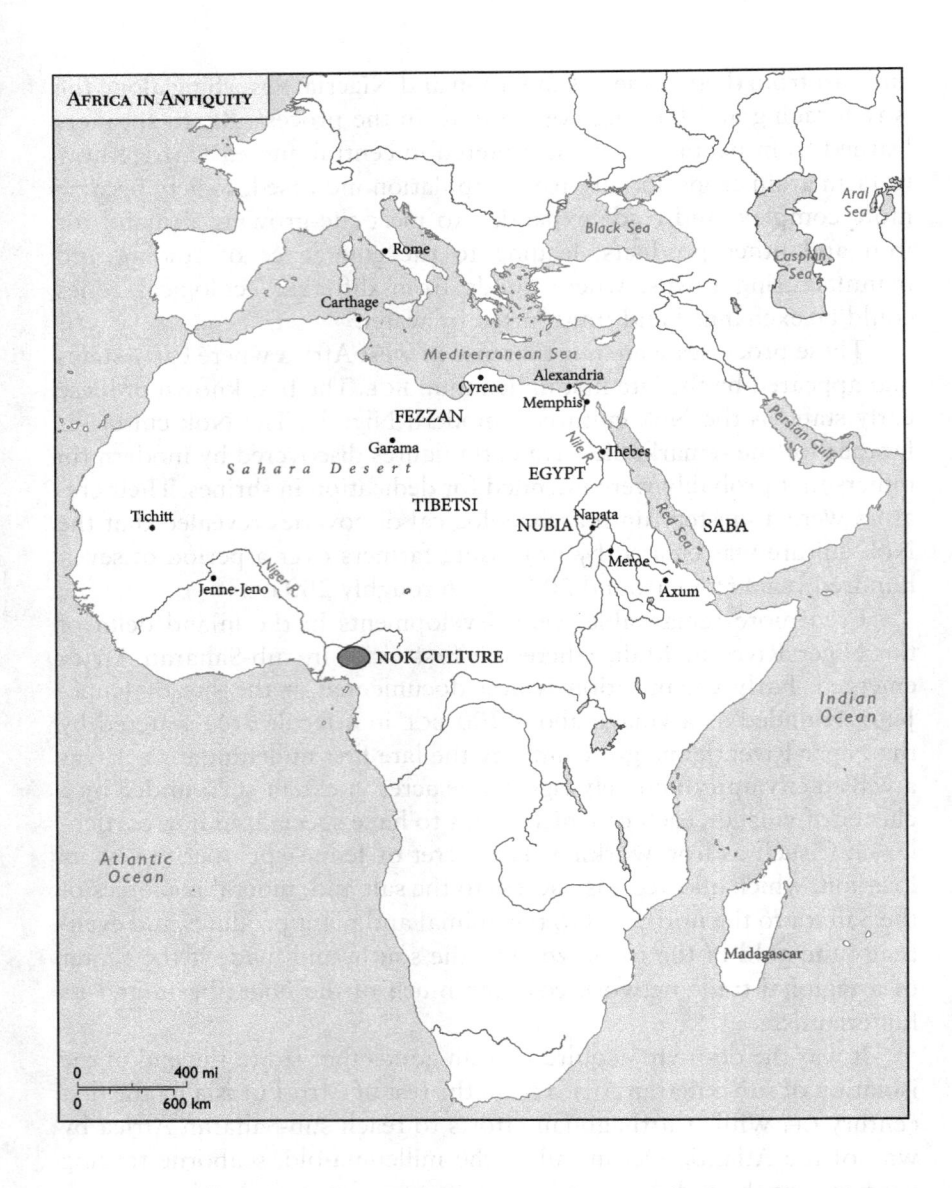

Not surprisingly, the integration of east Africa into the Indian Ocean trading network also transformed political relations in northeast

Africa. The Nile valley had been the primary route by which goods from the African interior reached Egypt and the Mediterranean since at least the third millennium BCE. However, the great increase in shipping in the Red Sea and Indian Ocean offered a more convenient route for these goods, and geography dictated that it would not be the landlocked kingdom of Kush but that of Aksum in the highlands of modern Ethiopia that benefited.

Unlike Kush, Aksum was of relatively recent origin. Although south Arabian colonists had founded a series of small kingdoms in what is now Eritrea and Ethiopia in the early first millennium BCE, Aksum first rose to prominence in the late first century BCE, when it became the capital of the kingdom of the Habasha or Abyssinians. Located on the Ethiopian plateau with ready access to the Upper Nile valley and its hinterlands on the west and to the Red Sea on the east, Aksum profited greatly from the expansion of trade in the Red Sea and Indian Ocean.

By the mid-first century CE Aksum was the principal center for the export of goods from the coastal regions of the Red Sea and surrounding area to the Mediterranean, Arabia, and south Asia. The second- and third-century CE Aksumite kings continued to support this trade, extending their rule over most of the hinterlands of the southern Red Sea basin and building and maintaining a caravan route to Egypt that bypassed the Nile corridor entirely, thereby confirming Aksum's rule as the principal supplier of northeast African goods to the Mediterranean basin.

Still, the late first century BCE and the first two centuries CE were in many ways the climax of Kushite history. Peaceful relations between Rome and Kush resulted in unprecedented prosperity. By the end of the third century CE, however, Kush was in decline. The emergence of Aksum as Rome's primary source of African goods gradually reduced diplomatic contact between Kush and Roman Egypt as Roman policy toward the Upper Nile valley increasingly focused on the defense of the southern frontier of Egypt. The weakening of the Kushite monarchy loosened its hold on its peripheral territories, exposing the kingdom to attack by its neighbors and ultimately conquest by Aksum. As a result, the Nile corridor ceased to be the principal artery for the transmission of African goods to Egypt, and Aksum became Rome's principal ally in Africa and the main intermediary between India and the Mediterranean basin in the Indian Ocean trade.

In contrast to the situation in east Africa, little is known about the early history of the trans-Saharan trade. The contents of the trade—sub-Saharan gold and slaves exchanged for Saharan salt and copper—leave no archaeological traces, so that scholars have dated it to the late first millennium CE when it is first mentioned in Arabic sources. The recent discovery of metal goods from Roman north Africa at Kissi in Burkina Faso[7] combined with discoveries in the territory of the kingdom of the Garamantes in the Fezzan indicate, however, that the trans-Saharan trade had already begun in the early centuries CE.

References to the Garamantes are numerous in Greek and Roman texts from the fifth century BCE to late antiquity. These suggest that as early as the fifth century BCE the Garamantes had already developed a state and were raiding sub-Saharan African populations for slaves, and that by the first century CE their kings' authority extended deep into the Sahara, perhaps even reaching the Sahel. Moreover, excavations at the Garamantian capital of Garama indicate that during the first three centuries CE the Garamantian kingdom occupied a large territory, used the Libyan script, maintained a massive irrigation-based agricultural system, and imported large amounts of luxury goods from Roman north Africa, probably in exchange for semi-precious stones, slaves, and wild animals for the Roman games. The size and wealth of the Garamantian kingdom, combined with the location of Garamantian fortifications and watchtowers on what are later known to be caravan routes toward the Niger bend and the Sahel, strongly suggest that this trade had already begun by the early centuries CE.

Inevitably, the growth in intercontinental trade was paralleled by increased contact between states from the Atlantic to the Pacific. Already at the beginning of the period the Roman Emperor Augustus boasted of receiving embassies from India and extending his protection over rulers from Britain to Iran. Farther east in central Asia, the Kushan emperors included among their titles the Indian Maharaja or Great King, the Chinese Son of Heaven, the Parthian King of Kings, and the Roman Caesar, reflecting the empire's continent-wide diplomatic and commercial contacts. Efforts made to establish direct contact, however, between Rome and China in order to exclude the Parthian intermediaries in the silk trade failed. The first attempt was in 97 CE, when an embassy dispatched to Rome by Ban Chao, the brother of the historian Ban Gu and Han governor of the Tarim basin, turned back before reaching its goal because of exaggerated information it received from the Parthians about the difficulties of the journey; and again in 166 CE, an embassy sent by the Roman emperor Marcus Aurelius reached the Later Han capital of Luoyang but failed to achieve the trade treaty it sought.[8]

Although the effort to establish diplomatic relations between Rome and Han China ultimately failed, the knowledge gained by merchants actually engaged in the Silk Road and Indian Ocean trades revolutionized geography in both empires. So, the second-century CE Alexandrian scholar Ptolemy synthesized Roman knowledge of Afro-Eurasia in his *Geography*, a work that included the principal stages of the caravan route to China and accounts of south and southeast Asia, and the east African coast as far south as Zanzibar, and served as the foundation of western and Islamic geography until the sixteenth century CE. At the same time, around 125 CE, the Chinese scholar Ban Yong, another member of the Ban family that included his father Ban Chao and his uncle Ban Gu, compiled *The Treatise on the Western Regions* for the Han Emperor An. This was an account of the various peoples from central Asia to the eastern Mediterranean that remained authoritative until the fifth century CE when it was incorporated into the *Hou Hanshu*, the official history of the Later Han Dynasty.

The connectivity that had marked the early centuries CE declined sharply in the third century CE, however. The reasons are complex, but one stands out: the abrupt end of the political and natural conditions that had provided the security that had made the globalization of these centuries possible. As in other periods of globalization, increased contact and interaction between previously isolated peoples without immunity to new diseases also brought with it vulnerability to pandemics such as the plague, probably smallpox, whose effect was felt from China to Rome. The epidemic was particularly serious in the west, where the plague entered the Roman Empire in the mid-160s CE with the return of an army from Parthia and recurred at irregular intervals for almost a century until the mid-third century CE.

Documentation concerning the plague's severity comparable to that available for the medieval bubonic plague is lacking. However, Chinese accounts of the plague, the Roman historian Dio Cassius's report[9] that two thousand people a day died in Rome at the peak of the epidemic, and known mortality rates from later smallpox outbreaks combine to suggest that the epidemic ultimately may have claimed as many as six million people or approximately 10 percent of the population of the Roman Empire and an untold number of people beyond its borders, leaving many of the affected areas depopulated in its wake, particularly those along the empire's northern and western frontiers. Like their Han contemporaries, the Romans sought to repopulate such areas by settling in them tribal peoples—German in their case—from beyond the frontier, a policy that probably seemed expedient but over the long term in both cases resulted in the loss of imperial control over Rome's frontier zones.

Although the results of the new frontier policy did not become apparent for centuries, the plague itself was an unanticipated consequence of a fundamental change in the political environment of Afro-Eurasia that defined its history until the Arab conquests of the seventh century CE: the collapse of Augustus's Parthian settlement in the early second century CE. The pretext for the renewal of war between Rome and Parthia was Parthia's attempt to install a pro-Parthian king in Armenia. The Roman response was initially more successful than the Emperor Trajan could have imagined. For a brief moment in 116 CE Roman power reached the Persian Gulf, and the goal of annexing Parthia that had tantalized Romans since Marcus Crassus's disastrous defeat in 54 BCE seemed within reach. In the end, however, it proved to be beyond Rome's power to retain its conquests in Mesopotamia, but tension with Parthia continued throughout the century with new outbreaks of hostilities in the 160s CE and the late 190s CE. While Parthia survived the Roman assaults, the cumulative effect of a century of tension and warfare was to weaken the kingdom and leave it vulnerable to repeated rebellions that climaxed in 224 CE, when a certain Ardashir, a member of a family of hereditary Zorastrian fire priests in the province of Persis, overthrew Artabanus IV, the last Parthian king, and founded a new Persian Empire that historians call the Sasanian Empire.

Sometimes history does repeat itself. Like Cyrus II and Cambyses, the founders of the first Persian Empire seven centuries earlier, Ardashir and his son Shapur I transformed, in a little under half a century, the weakened Parthian kingdom into a superpower that extended from Mesopotamia in the west to northwest India in the east, in the process stripping the Kushan Empire of the bulk of its territories. Hardest hit by the sudden emergence of a powerful new Persian Empire, however, was Rome. Three unsuccessful Roman attempts to fend off Sasanian expansion westward into Syria in 235 CE, 244 CE, and 260 CE ended disastrously. The Roman Emperor Valerian was captured and taken to Persia where his stuffed body was later displayed to shocked Roman ambassadors, and Antioch—the third largest city of the empire—was sacked and its skilled craftsmen were deported to Persia to work for Shapur I. Only a timely defeat inflicted on the Persian forces by Odenath, the ruler of Palmyra, averted the complete collapse of Rome's eastern frontier.

The repercussions of the unexpected appearance of a new superpower on Rome's eastern frontier and her inadequate response to the new threat affected the empire for the rest of the third century CE. The most obvious result was unprecedented political instability as

A relief depicting the Sasanian Persian emperor Shapur I accepting the surrender of the Roman emperor Valerian in 260 CE. The selection of Naqsh-i Rustam, the site of the tombs of the ancient kings of Persia, for this artistic celebration of Shapur's victory over Rome reflects the claim of the Sasanian kings to be the successors of the ancient kings of Persia. Shutterstock 365798417

twenty-two emperors held the imperial throne during the half-century between 235 CE and 284 CE. More fundamental, however, was the transformation of life in free Germany as the weakening of Rome's western frontier defenses by the transfer of forces to the east to counter the new Persian threat or their involvement in civil wars over succession to the imperial throne offered German tribes the possibility of seizing new territories and acquiring wealth by looting the empire and its allies.

As a result, whole German tribes migrated southeastward from their homes in Poland to the steppes north of the Black Sea where they reappeared reorganized into the powerful tribal confederation the Romans later called the Goths; most important, they were possessed of sufficient military power to challenge the weakened frontier garrisons. Comparable developments occurred farther west along the Rhine and Danube frontiers where similar confederations known as the Alamanni and the Franks absorbed many of the small German tribes described by Tacitus in the late first century CE. From Gaul to the Aegean, forces of the new German confederations raided and looted cities, undoing centuries of urban development in the process.

CRISIS AND RECOVERY   119

At the peak of the crisis in the 260s CE and early 270s CE the Roman emperor ruled little more than Italy, north Africa, and the Balkans. In the west, the provinces of Spain, Gaul, and Britain had seceded and formed a separate Roman-style empire, while in the east, Zenobia, the queen of Palmyra, who claimed to be a descendant of the great Cleopatra, had seized control of Rome's provinces from Anatolia to Egypt. The very survival of the empire must have seemed in doubt so that its almost total restoration in little more than a decade must have astonished contemporaries; this transformation was brought about by a remarkable series of military emperors beginning with the accession of Aurelian in 270 CE and ending with that of Diocletian in 284 CE.

Appearances were deceiving, however. Although the territorial integrity of the empire was restored with only minor losses—the most notable of which was Dacia, modern Romania, which Aurelian abandoned after a little more than a century and a half of Roman rule—the Republican façade so carefully constructed by Augustus had disappeared and the restored empire resembled in many ways its eastern contemporaries, the Sasanian and Chinese empires. The emperor was no longer *Princeps*, first citizen, but a sacral monarch who resided in a sacred palace surrounded by eunuchs and separated from his subjects by elaborate protocol, claiming to be the link between the gods and mankind. The bureaucracy expanded greatly to support the reorganized government, while the army took over many of the local governmental functions that had been performed by the urban elite before it was decimated in the chaos of the third century CE. Not even so conservative an institution as the Roman army was immune to change, as Persian-style heavy armored cavalry units known as *cataphracts* that were composed of mercenary troopers recruited from Iranian-speaking nomads known as Sarmatians multiplied to cope with the Sasanian threat.

These changes were not planned but developed piecemeal in the course of the empire's struggle to survive until they were finally consolidated and systematized by the Emperor Diocletian during his two-decade-long reign from 284 CE to 305 CE. Diocletian was also responsible for a change in the organization of the empire that determined the course of its future history. Faced with serious and continuing threats on both its eastern and western frontiers, Diocletian divided the empire administratively, appointing, in the words of the Christian scholar Lactantius, "three men to share his rule, dividing the world into four parts and multiplying the armies since each of the four strove to have a far larger number of troops than previous emperors had had when they were governing the state alone."[10] The four co-rulers mentioned by

Lactantius were not equal, however, since the system as a whole was overseen by two senior emperors or Augusti, one for the Latin-speaking western half of the empire and one for the more populous and wealthier Greek-speaking eastern half. Not surprisingly, Diocletian assigned the latter position to himself.

Diocletian's division of the empire into two halves survived and became the norm during the remaining two centuries of its existence. Although an understandable response to the empire's immediate military problems, the division of the empire seriously disadvantaged the western emperors, who had to defend longer and more exposed frontiers with fewer resources than their eastern co-rulers. An even more profound long-term effect was the intensification of the cultural differences between the two halves of the empire, so that by the fifth century CE even a well-educated intellectual living in the western half of the Roman Empire like St. Augustine no longer had the knowledge of Greek or Greek literature that had been routine among educated Romans of the late Republic or early Empire like Julius Caesar or the poet Virgil.

The repercussions of the Sasanian conquest of the Parthian and Kushan empires were also felt in south Asia. With the disappearance of the stabilizing influence of the Kushans, India fragmented into multiple petty kingdoms continuously at war with each other in the hope of occupying pieces of the defunct Kushan Empire. How many kingdoms were involved is unknown but Chandra Gupta I's claim to have conquered fourteen kings in south India alone gives a clear idea of the extent of the fragmentation that existed before the establishment of the Gupta Empire in the 320s CE restored stability to north and central India. Although the accession of Chandra Gupta I, who favored Brahminism, marked the end of the imperial patronage Buddhism had enjoyed under the Kushans, the cultural trends of the Kushan era continued after the fall of the empire as revealed by the spread of Gandhara-style art throughout central and east Asia, the construction of numerous stupas and other Buddhist monuments in India, and the flourishing state of Buddhist scholarship that would attract Chinese Buddhist monks such as Faxian, who traveled to India in the early fifth century CE and spent thirteen years visiting Buddhist sacred sites and collecting accurate copies of Buddhist texts.

Globalization, even the limited globalization of the first two centuries CE, meant that China also did not remain unaffected by events farther west. Ban Yong's detailed accounts of states from central Asia to the Mediterranean and reports of visits to China of embassies from them from the first century CE to the third century CE are clear evidence of China's growing involvement in the affairs of Afro-Eurasia. By the mid-second century CE, however, China also had begun to be affected by the deterioration of conditions beyond her northern frontier. As happened in contemporary Rome, the first sign of trouble was the outbreak of plague in the 160s CE in China's military, which weakened her ability to defend her frontiers. At the same time, the Greek travel writer Pausanias reported that silk came from an island in the south, indicating an increase in seaborne transport of silk to the west, as insecurity in central Asia led to a decline in the lucrative caravan trade.[11]

The decline of the caravan trade and the revenues it produced made it increasingly difficult to maintain China's position in central Asia so that by the time the Later Han Dynasty disappeared in 220 CE, China's northern frontier had collapsed and Chinese authority beyond the Great Wall was only a memory. Events in China during the following sixty years eerily parallel those in contemporary Rome. As the title of one of the masterpieces of Chinese literature, *The Romance of the Three Kingdoms*, indicates, China fragmented into three rival states ruled by warlord families: Wei in the Yellow River Valley, Wu in the Yangtze River Valley and the southern coastal cities, and Shu in southwestern China. Chronic warfare, whose effects were worsened by the pillaging of nomad mercenaries recruited by the kingdoms to compensate for the losses in manpower caused by the plague, crippled agriculture and spurred immigration south into the kingdoms of Wu and Shu, thereby hastening the process of culturally integrating the south into the mainstream of Chinese culture. Meanwhile, efforts to introduce a merit system for administrative appointments failed, reinforcing the monopoly of government service by the landed aristocracy that had begun under the Later Han Dynasty. And then, almost as unexpectedly as happened in contemporary Rome, the Jin Dynasty, which was founded by a warlord family named Sima, reunited China by first seizing control of Shu in 263 CE, then Wei two years later, and finally Wu in 280 CE.

The crisis of the third century CE had shaken the foundations of the global order from the Atlantic to the Pacific. Recovery was uneven, but by 300 CE the worst was over. Although the Jin Dynasty would collapse shortly after the turn of the century, and China would fragment again for almost three centuries before being reunited again by the Sui Dynasty, the Sassanid and Roman empires would provide stability from central Asia to the Mediterranean, thereby establishing the basic political framework that would govern affairs in Afro-Eurasia until the Arab conquests of the seventh century CE. Renewed stability even allowed restoration of trade between the east and the west both along the Silk Roads and via the Indian Ocean and the Persian Gulf and the Red Sea.

Beneath the surface, however, society was very different at the beginning of the fourth century CE from the way it had been a century earlier. A new social order was forming, one that was dominated by landed aristocracies, who were patrons of peasantries increasingly bound to the land they worked. Governments that were too weak to resist these developments despite their autocratic pretensions acquiesced, incorporating the aristocrats' usurped privileges into law. In China this was done by assigning extra points for high birth to the rankings used for appointments to government office and in Rome by making the distinction between aristocrats and non-aristocrats the basis of legal process. At the same time, the cultural divide between the new Roman and Chinese aristocracies and their Germanic and central Asian enemies gradually eroded, as elite military units increasingly were composed of mercenaries recruited from beyond the boundaries of the empires. Most profound in their long-term repercussions on the development of culture and society, however, were new religions closely allied to the state that were based on canonical sacred books that preserved the teachings of inspired religious leaders.

Such religions first became a central feature of Afro-Eurasian life in the third century CE when Zoroastrianism became the state religion of the Sasanian Empire, thanks to the work of a fire priest named Kartir. Supported by Shapur I and his immediate successors, Kartir codified the text of the Avesta and established an extensive network of priests and fire temples covering the whole empire, while organizing state-sponsored persecutions of potential rival religions including Judaism, Hinduism, Buddhism, Manichaeism, and Christianity.

Religious persecution was not limited to the Sasanian Empire. Christians also were being persecuted in the Roman Empire, not sporadically as Perpetua and her friends had been at the beginning of the third century CE, but systematically throughout the empire as the Emperor Diocletian strove to eradicate Christianity once and for all. Yet a little over a decade later Christianity would be recognized as the state religion of the kingdom of Armenia, and the Roman emperor Constantine, who had converted to Christianity in 307 CE, would openly proclaim his support for the religion in the so-called Edict of Milan. These events marked the end of three turbulent centuries during which Christianity had survived the execution of its founding figure, Jesus; its divorce from Judaism after the great Jewish revolt of 66 to 70 CE; and increasingly severe persecution by the Roman government in the third century CE. By the time Diocletian launched the last and harshest persecution in early 303 CE, Christianity was no longer an obscure cult but an empire-wide religious community governed by a clergy whose organization extended from lowly village priests to powerful bishops located in the major cities of the empire.

The spread of Zoroastrianism and Christianity was revolutionary. From central Asia to the Atlantic the intellectual and artistic cultures of antiquity either gradually ended or were radically transformed. In the Sasanian Empire, Zoroastrian priests created a new Pahlavi literature that included not only theological and scientific texts influenced by Greek and Indian works but also heroic sagas that influenced some of the greatest writers of medieval Persian literature. Similarly, by 300 CE Christianity already had given birth to an extensive and varied literature in both Greek and Latin that drew on Greek philosophy and literature to defend Christian teaching against its critics. In so doing it made possible the survival of much of Greek and Latin literature to the present. Nevertheless, the fact remains that only those aspects of ancient intellectual and artistic culture survived that could be reconciled with the new religions. Perpetua would probably have been satisfied with that result.

Chronology

1177 BCE
Defeat of the Sea Peoples by Ramses III

1069 BCE
End of the Egyptian New Kingdom

1045 BCE
Shang Dynasty overthrown by the Western Zhou

CA. 800–CA. 580s BCE
Phoenician colonization in the Mediterranean

771 BCE
Fall of the Western Zhou Dynasty

771–256 BCE
Eastern Zhou Dynasty

CA. 750–CA. 500 BCE
Greek colonization in the Mediterranean and Black Sea

747–656 BCE
Egypt ruled by the Kushite Twenty-Fifth Dynasty

745–612 BCE
The Neo-Assyrian Empire

722–481 BCE
Spring and Autumn period in China

695 BCE
Cimmerian invasion of Anatolia

612 BCE
Medes and Babylonians overthrow the Assyrian Empire

CA. 599–525 BCE
Life of Mahavira

CA. 563–483 BCE
Life of the Buddha

559–529 BCE
Reign of Cyrus II of Persia

CA. 551–CA. 479 BCE
Life of Confucius

CA. 500 BCE–CA. 200 CE
Nok Culture in west Africa

CA. 484–CA. 414 BCE
Life of Herodotus

481–221 BCE
Warring States period in China

480–479 BCE
Persian invasion of Greece

431–404 BCE
Peloponnesian War

399 BCE
Trial and execution of Socrates

336–323 BCE
Reign of Alexander the Great

323–281 BCE
Fragmentation of Alexander's empire

CA. 321–CA. 297 BCE
Reign of Chandragupta Maurya

312–63 BCE
Seleucid Kingdom in Asia

304–30 BCE
Ptolemaic Kingdom in Egypt

CA. 269–CA. 232 BCE
Reign of Ashoka

247 BCE–224 CE
Rise and fall of Parthia

264–146 BCE
The Punic Wars

221–206 BCE
Unification of China under the Qin Dynasty

200–30 BCE
Roman conquest of the eastern Mediterranean

202 BCE–9 CE
Western Han Dynasty

184 BCE
Foundation of the Shunga Dynasty in India

175–161 BCE
Xiongnu defeat and drive Yuezhi toward central Asia

CA. 145–86 BCE
Life of Sima Qian

128 BCE
Zhang Qian reports on conditions in Bactria

58–51 BCE
Roman conquest of Gaul

CA. 45–CA. 260 CE
Rise and fall of the Kushan Empire

30 BCE–14 CE
Reign of Augustus

9 CE
Rome withdraws from Germany

25–200 CE
Eastern Han Dynasty

CA. 50 CE
Compilation of the *Periplus of the Erythraean Sea*

CA. 129–152 CE
Kanishka patronizes Buddhism in Kushan territory

CA. 166 CE
First direct contact between Rome and China

224 CE
Ardashir founds the Sasanian Persian Empire

266–280 CE
Jin Dynasty reunites China

274 CE
Death of Mani

284–305 CE
Reign of Diocletian

Notes

PREFACE

1. Mani, *Kephalaia*, Persia 189.1, in Ian Gardner, *The Kephalaia of the Teacher: The Edited Coptic Manichaean Texts in Translation with Commentary* (Leiden: E. J. Brill, 1995).
2. Seneca, *Medea*, lines 376–380, in Seneca, *Tragedies*, edited and translated by Frank Justus Miller, vol. 1 (Cambridge, MA: Harvard University Press, 1917).
3. In Greek mythology Tethys is the daughter of Earth and the sister and wife of Ocean and the mother of rivers and the sea nymphs.
4. Thule was the northernmost land known to the Greeks and Romans, possibly to be identified with Scandinavia or modern Iceland.

CHAPTER 1

1. "The War against the Peoples of the Sea," translated by John A. Wilson, in *Ancient Near Eastern Texts Relating to the Old Testament*, edited by James B. Pritchard, 2nd edition (Princeton, NJ: Princeton University Press, 1955), 262.
2. Climate change as a factor in the crisis was brought to historians' attention by Rhys Carpenter, *Discontinuity in Greek Civilization* (Cambridge: Cambridge University Press, 1968).
3. "The Report of Wenamun," in Miriam Lichtheim, *Ancient Egyptian Literature*, vol. 2, *The New Kingdom* (Berkeley: University of California Press, 1976), 226.
4. "The Babylonian Theodicy," translated by Robert D. Biggs, in *The Ancient Near East: Supplementary Texts and Pictures Relating to the Old Testament*, edited by James B. Pritchard (Princeton, NJ: Princeton University Press, 1969), 603.
5. For a lucid survey of current scholarship on the historical value of the Bible see Daniel C. Snell, "Syria-Palestine in Recent Research," in *Current Issues in the Study of the Ancient Near East*, edited by Mark W. Chavalas (Claremont, CA: Regina Books, 2007), 113–149.
6. *The Rig Veda: An Anthology*, translated by Wendy Doniger (London: Penguin Books, 1981), 31.
7. Valerie Hansen, *The Open Empire: A History of China to 1600* (New York: W. W. Norton, 2000), 27.

CHAPTER 2

1. Hesiod, *Works and Days*, line 493, in David W. Tandy and Walter C. Neale, *Hesiod's Works and Days* (Berkeley: University of California Press, 1996), 105.
2. Plato, *Critias* 110 b5. Translation by the author.
3. 1 Kings 5:1–12; 10:11–22, in *The Oxford Study Bible: Revised English Bible with the Apocrypha*, edited by M. Jack Suggs, Katherine Doob Sakenfeld, and James R. Mueller (Oxford: Oxford University Press, 1992), 347, 356.
4. Ezekiel 27:33, in *The Oxford Study Bible*, 886.
5. Sappho, Fragment 16, in *Greek Lyric*, vol. 1, translated by David A. Campbell (Cambridge, MA: Harvard University Press, 1982), 66.

6. "Babylonian and Assyrian Historical Texts," translated by A. Leo Oppenheim in *Ancient Near Eastern Texts Relating to the Old Testament*, edited by James B. Pritchard, 2nd edition (Princeton, NJ: Princeton University Press, 1955), 290–291.
7. "Babylonian and Assyrian Historical Texts," translated by A. Leo Oppenheim in *Ancient Near Eastern Texts*, 284–285.
8. Quoted in Neil MacGregor, *A History of the World in 100 Objects* (New York: Viking, 2010), 149.

CHAPTER 3

1. Simo Parpola, ed., *Letters from Assyrian and Babylonian Scholars, State Archives of Assyria*, vol. 10 (Helsinki: Helsinki University Press, 1993), 89.
2. Herodotus, *Histories* 1.106, in Herodotus, *The Histories*, translated by Walter Blanco, 2nd ed. (New York: W. W. Norton, 2013).
3. Robert Drews, *Early Riders: The Beginnings of Mounted Warfare in Asia and Europe* (New York: Routledge, 2004), 65–74.
4. The remarkable finds at Pazyrik were published in Sergei I. Rudenko, *Frozen Tombs of Siberia: The Pazyryk Burials of Iron-Age Horseman*, translated by M. W. Thompson (Berkeley: University of California Press, 1970).
5. Translated in *Papyrus and Tablet*, edited by A. Kirk Grayson and Donald B. Redford (Englewood Cliffs, NJ: 1973), 110.
6. Translated in *Papyrus and Tablet*, 111.
7. Nahum, 3:18–19, in *The Oxford Study Bible: Revised English Bible with the Apocrypha*, edited by M. Jack Suggs, Katherine Doob Sakenfeld, and James R. Mueller (Oxford: Oxford University Press, 1992), 974.
8. Isaiah, 45: 1 in *The Oxford Study Bible*, 753.
9. Diodorus, *Library of History*, 12.1–2, in D. Brendan Nagle and Stanley M. Burstein, *Readings in Greek History: Sources and Interpretations*, 2nd ed. (New York: Oxford University Press, 2014).
10. DSf 3e and 3i in Roland G. Kent, *Old Persian: Grammar, Texts, Lexicon* (New Haven, CT: American Oriental Society, 1953), 144.
11. Thucydides, *The Peloponnesian War*, translated by Walter Blanco (New York: W. W. Norton, 1998), 3.82.2.
12. Quoted with adaptation from Cho-yun Hsu, "The Spring and Autumn Period," in *The Cambridge History of Ancient China: From the Origins of Civilization to 221 B.C.*, edited by Michael Loewe and Edward L. Shaughnessy (Cambridge: Cambridge University Press, 1999), 557.

CHAPTER 4

1. Isocrates, *To Philip* 132, in *Isocrates*, translated by George Norlin, vol. 1 (Cambridge, MA: Harvard University Press, 1928).
2. Thucydides, *The Peloponnesian War*, translated by Walter Blanco (New York: W. W. Norton, 1998), 1.10.2.
3. Thucydides, *The Peloponnesian War*, 1.1.1.
4. *The Constitution of Athens* by "The Old Oligarch," translated by H. G. Dakyns in *The Greek Historians*, edited by Francis R. B. Godolphin, vol. 2 (New York: Random House, 1942), 638.
5. Thucydides, *The Peloponnesian War*, 2.53.
6. Plato, *Epistles*, translated by Glenn R. Morrow (Indianapolis: Bobbs-Merrill, 1962), 7, 328c.

7. Diodorus, *Library of History*, 18.1.4, in D. Brendan Nagle and Stanley M. Burstein, *Readings in Greek History: Sources and Interpretations*, 2nd ed. (New York: Oxford University Press, 2014).
8. Plato, *Phaedo* 109b.
9. Quoted in Naphtali Lewis, *Greeks in Ptolemaic Egypt: Case Studies in the Social History of the Hellenistic World* (Oxford: Clarendon Press, 1986), 85.
10. The clearest introduction to the new scholarship on the Septuagint is Tessa Rajak, *Translation and Survival: The Greek Bible of the Ancient Jewish Diaspora* (Oxford: Oxford University Press, 2009).
11. Ashoka, *Rock Edict XIII*, in *The Edicts of Asoka*, edited and translated by N. A. Nikam and Richard McKeon (Chicago: University of Chicago Press, 1959), 27.
12. *Rock Edict II*, in *The Edicts of Asoka*, 64.
13. Li Feng, *Early China: A Social and Cultural History* (Cambridge: Cambridge University Press, 2013), 186–187.
14. Quoted in Arthur Waley, *Three Ways of Thought in Ancient China* (Stanford, CA: Stanford University Press, 1982), 58.
15. *Hanfeizei*, translated by Robin R. Wang, in *Images of Women in Chinese Thought and Culture: Writings from the Pre-Qin Period through the Song Dynasty*, edited by Robin R. Wang (Indianapolis: Hackett, 2003), 122.

CHAPTER 5

1. There is a translation of Sima Qian's summary of Zhang Qian's report in *Records of the Grand Historian: Chapters from the SHIH CHI of Ssu-ma Ch'ien*, translated by Burton Watson (New York: Columbia University Press, 1969), 274–280.
2. The Yuezhi were nomads who probably spoke Tocharian, an Indo-European language that is known primarily from Buddhist manuscripts discovered in the Tarim Basin early in the twentieth century by the explorer Aurel Stein.
3. Polybius, *The Histories* 5.104, translated by Robin Waterfield (Oxford: Oxford University Press, 2010).
4. Virgil, *The Aeneid* 4, lines 474–478, translated by Robert Fagles (New York: Viking, 2006).
5. Polybius, *The Histories* 1.1, translated by Robin Waterfield.
6. Horace, *Epistles* 2, 1, lines 156–157. Translation by author.
7. There is a recent translation of the Hathigumpha inscription in Romila Thapar, *Early India: From the Origins to AD 1300* (Berkeley: University of California Press, 2002), 212–213.
8. *The Arthaśāstra: Selections from the Classic Indian Work on Statecraft*, edited and translated by Mark McClish and Patrick Olivelle (Indianapolis: Hackett, 2012), 121.
9. *The Questions of King Milinda*, translated by T. W. Rhys Davids, vol. 1 (Oxford: Oxford University Press, 1890), 2–3.
10. Liu Yiqing, *A New Account of Tales of the World*, translated by Richard Mather, in *Images of Women in Chinese Thought and Culture: Writings from the Pre-Qin Period through the Song Dynasty*, edited by Robin R. Wang (Indianapolis: Hackett, 2003), 212.

CHAPTER 6

1. Sima Qian, "Letter to Ren An," translated by Ivy Sui-yuen, in Thomas R. Martin, *Herodotus and Sima Qian: The First Great Historians of Greece and China, a Brief History with Documents* (Boston: Bedford/St. Martin's, 2010), 85–93.

2. John E. Hill, *Through the Jade Gate to Rome: A Study of the Silk Routes during the Later Han Dynasty 1st to 2nd Centuries CE, an Annotated Translation of the Chronicle on the "Western Regions" in the Hou Hanshu* (private publication, 2009), 23.
3. Virgil, *Aeneid* 1, line 279, translated by Robert Fagles (New York: Viking, 2006).
4. Tacitus, *Germania* 33, in Tacitus, *Agricola and Germany*, translated by A. R. Birley (Oxford: Oxford University Press, 1999).
5. Augustus, *Res Gestae Divi Augusti* 34. Translation by author.
6. Tacitus, *Annals* 1.3. Translation by author.
7. Juvenal, *Satires* 3, line 60. Translation by author.
8. "Stele of Sophytos, Son of Naratos," in D. Brendan Nagle and Stanley M. Burstein, *Readings in Greek History: Sources and Interpretations*, 2nd ed. (New York: Oxford University Press, 2014), 307.
9. *Pañcatantra* 5.26, in Visnu Śarma, *The Pañcatantra*, translated by Chandra Rajan (Middlesex, England: Penguin, 1995).
10. *The Laws of Manu*, translated by Wendy Doniger with Brian K. Smith (Middlesex, England: Penguin, 1991), 10.81–82.
11. James A. Millward, *The Silk Road: A Very Short Introduction* (Oxford: Oxford University Press, 2013), 24.
12. Ban Zhao, *Lessons for Women*, translated by Robin R. Wang, in *Images of Women in Chinese Thought and Culture: Writings from the Pre-Qin Period through the Song Dynasty*, edited by Robin R. Wang (Indianapolis: Hackett, 2003), 179.
13. Tacitus, *Annals* 4.32. Translation by author.

CHAPTER 7

1. Perpetua's diary is translated in Joyce E. Salisbury, *Perpetua's Passion: The Death and Memory of a Young Roman Woman* (London: Routledge, 1997).
2. Marcus Aurelius, *Meditations* 11.3.
3. Edward Gibbon, *The History of the Decline and Fall of the Roman Empire*, edited by David Womersley, vol. 1 (London: Penguin, 1994), 103.
4. Tacitus, *Agricola* 21. Translation by author.
5. Pliny, *Natural History* 6.54. Translation by author.
6. *The Periplus Maris Erythraei: Text with Introduction, Translation, and Commentary* by Lionel Casson (Princeton, NJ: Princeton University Press, 1989), 49.
7. The discoveries at Kissi and their significance are discussed in *Crossroads / Carrefour Sahel: Cultural and Technological Developments in First Millennium BC/AD West Africa*, edited by Sonja Magnavita, Lassina Koté, Peter Breunig, and Oumarou A. Idé, *Journal of African Archaeology Monograph Series*, vol. 2 (Frankfurt am Main: Africa Magna Verlag, 2009), 79–146.
8. John E. Hill, *Through the Jade Gate to Rome: A Study of the Silk Routes during the Later Han Dynasty 1st to 2nd Centuries CE, an Annotated Translation of the Chronicle on the "Western Regions" in the Hou Hanshu* (private publication, 2009), 27.
9. Dio Cassius, *Roman History* 72.14.3–4.
10. Lactantius, *On the Death of the Persecutors* 7.1, translated by J. L. Creed (Oxford: Oxford University Press, 1984), quoted in *Readings in Late Antiquity: A Sourcebook*, edited by Michael Maas (London: Routledge, 2000), 12.
11. Pausanias, *Description of Greece* 6.26.9–10.

Further Reading

GENERAL WORKS

Bang, Peter Fibiger, and Walter Scheidel, eds. *The Oxford Handbook of the State in the Ancient Near East and Mediterranean.* Oxford: Oxford University Press, 2013.

Beckwith, Christopher I. *Empires of the Silk Road: A History of Central Eurasia from the Bronze Age to the Present.* Princeton, NJ: Princeton University Press, 2009.

Bellah, Robert N., and Hans Joas, eds. *The Axial Age and Its Consequences.* Cambridge, MA: Harvard University Press, 2012.

Benjamin, Craig, ed. *The Cambridge World History.* Vol. 4, *A World with States, Empires, and Networks, 1200 BCE–900 CE.* Cambridge: Cambridge University Press, 2015.

Cunliffe, Barry. *By Steppe, Desert, and Ocean: The Birth of Eurasia.* Oxford: Oxford University Press, 2015.

Cunliffe, Barry. *Europe between the Oceans: 9000 BC–AD 1000.* New Haven, CT: Yale University Press, 2008.

Daryaee, Touraj, ed. *The Oxford Handbook of Iranian History.* Oxford: Oxford University Press, 2012.

Feng, Li. *Early China: A Social and Cultural History.* Cambridge: Cambridge University Press, 2013.

Fernández-Armesto, Felipe. *Pathfinders: A Global History of Exploration.* New York: W. W. Norton, 2006.

Johnston, Sarah Iles, ed. *Ancient Religions.* Cambridge, MA: Harvard University Press, 2004.

Price, Simon, and Peter Thonemann. *The Birth of Classical Europe: A History from Troy to Augustine.* New York: Viking, 2011.

Talbert, Richard J. A., ed. *Barrington Atlas of the Greek and Roman World.* Princeton, NJ: Princeton University Press, 2000.

Thapar, Romila. *Early India: From the Origins to AD 1300.* Berkeley: University of California Press, 2004.

THE NEW WORLD OF THE EARLY FIRST MILLENNIUM BCE (CA. TWELFTH–ELEVENTH CENTURIES BCE)

Cline, Eric H. *1177 B.C.: The Year Civilization Collapsed.* Princeton, NJ: Princeton University Press, 2014.

Dodson, Aidan. *Afterglow of Empire: Egypt from the Fall of the New Kingdom to the Saite Renaissance.* Cairo: American University in Cairo Press, 2012.

Drews, Robert. *The End of the Bronze Age: Changes in Warfare and the Catastrophe ca. 1200 B.C.* Princeton, NJ: Princeton University Press, 1993.

Liverani, Mario. *Israel's History and the History of Israel.* London: Equinox, 2005.

Lowe, Michael, and Edward L. Shaughnessy, eds. *The Cambridge History of Ancient China: From the Origins of Civilization to 221 B.C.* Cambridge: Cambridge University Press, 1999.

Sandars, N. K. *The Sea Peoples: Warriors of the Ancient Mediterranean.* 2nd ed. London: Thames and Hudson, 1985.

Thomas, Carol G., and Craig Conant. *Citadel to City-State: The Transformation of Greece, 1200–700 B.C.E.* Bloomington: Indiana University Press, 1999.

Welsby, Derek A. *The Kingdom of Kush: The Napatan and Meroitic Empires.* London: British Museum Press, 1996.

THE EARLY IRON AGE (CA. TENTH–SEVENTH CENTURIES BCE)

Aubet, Maria Eugenia. *The Phoenicians and the West: Politics, Colonies, and Trade.* 2nd ed. Cambridge: Cambridge University Press, 2001.

Basham, A. L. *The Wonder That Was India: A Survey of the Culture of the Indian Sub-Continent before the Coming of the Muslims.* New York: Macmillan, 1954.

Boardman, John. *The Greeks Overseas: Their Early Colonies and Trade.* 4th ed. London: Thames and Hudson, 1999.

Bottéro, Jean, Clarisse Herrenschmidt, and Jean-Pierre Vernant. *Ancestor of the West: Writing, Reasoning, and Religion in Mesopotamia, Elam, and Greece.* Translated by Teresa Lavender Fagan. Chicago: University of Chicago Press, 2000.

Bryce, Trevor. *The World of the Neo-Hittite Kingdoms: A Political and Military History.* Oxford: Oxford University Press, 2012.

Burkert, Walter. *The Orientalizing Revolution: Near Eastern Influence on Greek Culture in the Early Archaic Age.* Translated by Margaret E. Pinder and Walter Burkert. Cambridge, MA: Harvard University Press, 1992.

Oates, Joan. *Babylon.* 2nd ed. London: Thames and Hudson, 1986.

Saggs, H. W. F. *The Might that Was Assyria.* London: Sidgwick and Jackson, 1984.

Shapiro, H. A., ed. *The Cambridge Companion to Archaic Greece.* Cambridge: Cambridge University Press, 2007.

EAST MEETS WEST: THE RISE OF PERSIA (CA. SIXTH–FIFTH CENTURIES BCE)

Barker, Graeme, and Tom Rasmussen. *The Etruscans.* Oxford: Blackwell, 1998.

Brett, Michael, and Elizabeth Fentress. *The Berbers.* Oxford: Blackwell, 1996.

Briant, Pierre. *From Cyrus to Alexander: A History of the Persian Empire.* Translated by Peter T. Daniels. Winona Lake, IN: Eisenbrauns, 2002.

Davies, J. K. *Democracy and Classical Greece.* 2nd ed. Cambridge, MA: Harvard University Press, 1993.

Feldherr, Andrew, and Grant Hardy, eds. *The Oxford History of Historical Writing.* Vol. 1, *Beginnings to AD 600.* Oxford: Oxford University Press, 2011.

Lancel, Serge. *Carthage: A History.* Translated by Antonia Nevill. Oxford: Blackwell, 1995.

Lloyd, G. E. R. *The Ambitions of Curiosity: Understanding the World in Ancient Greece and China.* Cambridge: Cambridge University Press, 2002.

Osborne, Robin, ed. *Classical Greece: 500–323 BC.* Oxford: Oxford University Press, 2000.

Rolle, Renate. *The World of the Scythians.* Translated by F. G. Walls. Berkeley: University of California Press, 1989.

Sedlar, Jean W. *India and the Greek World: A Study in the Transmission of Culture.* Totowa, NJ: Rowman and Littlefield, 1980.

Wells, Peter S. *Farms, Villages, and Cities: Commerce and Urban Origins in Late Prehistoric Europe.* Ithaca, NY: Cornell University Press, 1984.

THE NEW WORLD OF THE MACEDONIAN KINGDOMS (CA. FOURTH–SECOND CENTURIES BCE)

Benjamin, Craig G. R. *The Yuezhi: Origin, Migration and the Conquest of Northern Bactria, Silk Road Studies.* Vol. 14. Turnhout, Belgium: Brepols, 2007.

Briant, Pierre. *Alexander the Great and His Empire.* Translated by Amélie Kuhrt. Princeton, NJ: Princeton University Press, 2010.

Bugh, Glenn R., ed. *The Cambridge Companion to the Hellenistic World.* Cambridge: Cambridge University Press, 2006.

Cosmo, Nicola Di. *Ancient China: The Rise of Nomadic Power in East Asian History.* Cambridge: Cambridge University Press, 2002.

Cunliffe, Barry. *The Extraordinary Voyage of Pytheas the Greek: The Man Who Discovered Britain.* London: Penguin Press, 2001.

Harris, William V. *War and Imperialism in Republican Rome: 327–70 B.C.* Oxford: Clarendon Press, 1979.

Kosmin, Paul J. *The Land of the Elephant Kings: Space, Territory, and Ideology in the Seleucid Empire.* Cambridge, MA: Harvard University Press, 2014.

Lewis, Naphtali. *Greeks in Ptolemaic Egypt.* Oxford: Clarendon Press, 1986.

Manning, J. G. *The Last Pharaohs: Egypt under the Ptolemies, 305–30 BC.* Princeton, NJ: Princeton University Press, 2010.

Salmons, Loren J., II., ed. *The Cambridge Companion to the Age of Pericles.* Cambridge: Cambridge University Press, 2007.

Sherwin-White, Susan, and Amélie Kuhrt. *From Samarkhand to Sardis: A New Approach to the Seleucid Empire.* London: Duckworth, 1993.

Thapar, Romila. *Aśoka and the Decline of the Mauryas.* 2nd ed. New Delhi: Oxford University Press, 1997.

Tritle, Lawrence A., ed. *The Greek World in the Fourth Century: From the Fall of the Athenian Empire to the Successors of Alexander.* London: Routledge, 1997.

Woolf, Greg. *Rome: An Empire's Story.* New York: Oxford University Press, 2012.

THE RISE OF THE PERIPHERIES: ROME AND CHINA (CA. THIRD–SECOND CENTURIES BCE)

Barclay, John M. G. *Jews in the Mediterranean Diaspora: From Alexander to Trajan (323 BCE–117 CE).* Berkeley: University of California Press, 1996.

Bickerman, Elias. *From Ezra to the Last of the Maccabees: Foundations of Post-biblical Judaism.* New York: Schocken Books, 1962.

Freeman, Philip. *The Philosopher and the Druids: A Journey among the Ancient Celts.* New York: Simon and Schuster, 2006.

Grajetski, Wolfram. *Greeks and Parthians in Mesopotamia and Beyond: 331 BC–224 AD.* London: Bristol Classical Press, 2011.

Gruen, Erich S. *Culture and National Identity in Republican Rome.* Ithaca, NY: Cornell University Press, 1992.

Lewis, Mark Edward. *The Early Chinese Empires: Qin and Han.* Cambridge, MA: Harvard University Press, 2007.

Mairs, Rachel. *The Hellenistic Far East: Archaeology, Language, and Identity in Greek Central Asia*. Berkeley: University of California Press, 2014.

Rajak, Tessa. *Translation and Survival: The Greek Bible of the Ancient Jewish Diaspora*. Oxford: Oxford University Press, 2009.

Waterfield, Robin. *Taken at the Flood: The Roman Conquest of Greece*. Oxford: Oxford University Press, 2014.

A NEW ORDER IN AFRO-EURASIA (CA. SECOND CENTURY BCE–SECOND CENTURY CE)

Auyang, Sunny Y. *The Dragon and the Eagle: The Rise and Fall of the Chinese and Roman Empires*. Armonk, NY: M. E. Sharpe, 2014.

Bispham, Edward, ed. *Roman Europe*. Oxford: Oxford University Press, 2008.

Burstein, Stanley M. *The Reign of Cleopatra*. Norman: University of Oklahoma Press, 2007.

Kim, Hyun Jin. *Ethnicity and Foreigners in Ancient Greece and China*. London: Duckworth, 2009.

Knapp, Robert. *Invisible Romans*. Berkeley: University of California Press, 2011.

Loewe, Michael. *The Government of the Qin and Han Empires: 221 BCE–220 CE*. Indianapolis: Hackett, 2006.

Millar, Fergus. *The Roman Near East: 31 BC–AD 337*. Cambridge, MA: Harvard University Press, 1993.

Parker, Grant. *The Making of Roman India*. Cambridge: Cambridge University Press, 2008.

Robinson, Richard H., and Willard L. Johnson. *The Buddhist Religion: A Historical Introduction*. 4th ed. Belmont, CA: Wadsworth, 1997.

Syme, Ronald. *The Roman Revolution*. Oxford: Clarendon Press, 1939.

Wells, Peter S. *The Barbarians Speak: How the Conquered Peoples Shaped Roman Europe*. Princeton. NJ: Princeton University Press, 1999.

Woolf, Greg. *Becoming Roman: The Origins of Provincial Civilization in Gaul*. Cambridge: Cambridge University Press, 1998.

CRISIS AND RECOVERY (THIRD CENTURY CE)

Daryaee, Touraj. *Sasanian Persia: The Rise and Fall of an Empire*. London: I. B. Tauris, 2010.

Ehret, Christopher. *An African Classical Age: Eastern and Southern Africa in World History, 1000 B.C. to A.D. 400*. Charlottesville: University Press of Virginia, 1998.

Groom, Nigel. *Frankincense and Myrrh: A Study of the Arabian Incense Trade*. London: Longman, 1981.

Hansen, Valerie. *The Silk Road: A New History*. New York: Oxford University Press, 2012.

Heather, Peter. *Empires and Barbarians: The Fall of Rome and the Birth of Europe*. Oxford: Oxford University Press, 2010.

Lewis, Mark Edward. *China between Empires: The Northern and Southern Dynasties*. Cambridge, MA: Harvard University Press, 2009.

Liu, Xinru. *Ancient India and Ancient China: Trade and Religious Exchanges AD 1–600*. New Delhi: Oxford University Press, 1988.

MacMullen, Ramsay. *Christianizing the Roman Empire (A.D. 100–400)*. New Haven, CT: Yale University Press, 1984.

McLaughlin, Raoul. *The Roman Empire and the Indian Ocean: The World Economy and the Kingdoms of Africa, Arabia and India*. Barnsley, UK: Pen and Sword, 2014.

Potter, David S. *The Roman Empire at Bay: AD 180–395*. London: Routledge, 2004.

Whittaker, C. R. *Rome and Its Frontiers: The Dynamics of Empire*. London: Routledge, 2004.

Wright, Arthur F. *Buddhism in Chinese History*. Stanford, CA: Stanford University Press, 1971.

Websites

ABZU
www.etana.org/abzubib
A portal that provides links to important websites and databases dealing with the history and culture of the ancient Near East and the ancient Mediterranean basin.

Ancient Greece
Ancient-greece.org/index.html
A portal containing links to numerous websites concerning Greek civilization, especially archaeology, art, and museums.

Ancient History Sourcebook
legacy.fordham.edu/Halsall/ancient/asbook.asp
A website containing a large selection of documents arranged thematically concerning the history of the ancient Near East, Egypt, Persia, Israel, Greece, and Rome.

Ancient India—The British Museum
http://www.ancientindia.co.uk
A broad-based introduction to the history and civilization of ancient India illustrated by relevant objects from the British Museum's extensive Indian collections.

The Ancient World Mapping Center
awmc.unc.edu
The website for the most important research institution in the United States for the study of ancient geography and cartography. In addition to information about the center, the site contains links to downloadable maps and other resources for studying the Greek and Roman world and its neighbors.

Asia for Educators
http://afe.easia.columbia.edu/
Comprehensive website and portal for teaching Asian civilization. Numerous links to museum sites dealing with Asian religion and art.

Digital Egypt for Universities
www.ucl.ac.uk/museums-static/digitalegyypt
Extensive resource for the study and teaching of the history of Egypt and Nubia from prehistory to 1000 CE.

Digital Roman Forum
dlib.etc.ucla.edu/projects/Forum
A detailed digital reconstruction of the Roman Forum as it existed around 400 CE.

Diotima
http://www.stoa.org/diotima/
A portal containing a comprehensive collection of links to websites, translated documents, and articles dealing with all aspects of the life of women in ancient Greece and Rome.

Electronic Resources for Classicists
www.tig.uci.edu/index/resources.html
A portal containing links to an extensive selection of online resources for research and teaching classics including databases, bibliographies, electronic journals, and teaching materials.

The Indian Ocean in World History Website
indianoceanhistory.org
A website treating the history of the Indian Ocean from prehistory to the present. It is structured around a chronological series of interactive maps that enables the study of economic and cultural interactions in the region.

Lacus Curtius: Into the Roman World
Penelope.uchicago.edu/Thayer/E/Roman/home
　A website devoted to Roman civilization. It contains an extensive selection of relevant Greek and Latin texts in both the original languages and translations and public-domain reference works.

Meroitic Database
meroiticdatabase.com
　Website focusing on information primarily concerning the Meroitic language but also providing links to the websites dealing with the archaeology and history of Kush.

ORBIS: The Stanford Geospatial Model of the Roman World
orbis.stanford.edu
　A website built around an interactive digital map of the Roman world that enables researchers to study communications by calculating distances and travel times between various locations within the Roman Empire.

Perseus Digital Library
http://www.perseus.tufts.edu
　The most extensive online resource for the study of ancient Greece and Rome. The site contains most extant Greek and Latin literature in both the original languages and translations together with grammars, dictionaries, and relevant reference works.

UCLA Encyclopedia of Egyptology
http://www.uee.ucla.edu
　Online encyclopedia dealing with all aspects of ancient Egyptian history and civilization.

A Visual Sourcebook of Chinese Civilization
https://depts.washington.edu/chinaciv/
　Extensive chronologically arranged website treating major themes of Chinese civilization including religion, technology, and material culture from prehistory to the present.

Acknowledgments

According to a familiar cliché, historians stand on the shoulders of their predecessors. That has been particularly true of the writing of this book, which is the result of more than half a century of study, teaching, and writing about ancient history. Virtually every sentence reflects that experience. I owe a particular debt of gratitude, however, to those individuals who generously gave of their time to read and comment on my manuscript. These included my colleagues Professors Ping Yao and Choi Chatterjee, Professors Frank L. Holt of the University of Houston and Caleb Finch of the University of Southern California, and Drs. D. Brendan Nagle and Robert W. Strayer, Professors Emeriti of the University of Southern California and the State University of New York at Brockport, respectively. Finally, I would also like to express my thanks to Nancy Toff, Alexandra Dauler, Elda Granata, and their staff at Oxford University Press and the editors of the New Oxford World History, Professors Bonnie Smith and Anand Yang, for their encouragement and support.

Pages 112 to 116 of this book are adapted and reprinted with permission from Stanley Burstein, "Africa: States, Empires, and Connections," in *The Cambridge World History*, vol. 4, *A World with States, Empires, and Networks, 1200 BCE—900 CE*, ed. Craig Benjamin (Cambridge: Cambridge University Press, 2015), 646–656.

NEW OXFORD WORLD HISTORY

The New Oxford World History

GENERAL EDITORS
BONNIE G. SMITH,
Rutgers University
ANAND A. YANG,
University of Washington

EDITORIAL BOARD
DONNA GUY,
Ohio State University
KAREN ORDAHL KUPPERMAN,
New York University
MARGARET STROBEL,
University of Illinois, Chicago
JOHN O. VOLL,
Georgetown University

The New Oxford World History provides a comprehensive, synthetic treatment of the "new world history" from chronological, thematic, and geographical perspectives, allowing readers to access the world's complex history from a variety of conceptual, narrative, and analytical viewpoints as it fits their interests.

Stanley M. Burstein is Professor Emeritus of History at California State University, Los Angeles. His field of research is Greek history with emphasis on relations between Greeks and non-Greeks. He is a former associate member of the American School of Classical Studies at Athens and a past president of the Association of Ancient Historians. He is the author of numerous books, including *Outpost of Hellenism: The Emergence of Heraclea on the Black Sea*; *The Babyloniaca of Berossus*; *The Hellenistic Age from the Battle of Ipsos to the Death of Kleopatra VII*; *Graeco-Africana: Studies in the History of Greek Relations with Egypt and Nubia*; *Ancient African Civilizations: Kush and Axum*; and *The Reign of Cleopatra*; and co-author of *Ancient Greece: A Political, Social and Cultural History*.

Chronological Volumes

The World from Beginnings to 4000 BCE
The World from 4000 to 1000 BCE
The World from 1000 BCE to 300 CE
The World from 300 to 1000 CE
The World from 1000 to 1500
The World from 1450 to 1700
The World in the Eighteenth Century
The World in the Nineteenth Century
The World in the Twentieth Century

Thematic and Topical Volumes

The City: A World History
Democracy: A World History
Empires: A World History
Food: A World History
The Family: A World History
Gender: A World History
Genocide: A World History
Health and Medicine: A World History
Migration: A World History
Race: A World History
Technology: A World History

Geographical Volumes

The Atlantic in World History
Central Asia in World History
China in World History
The Indian Ocean in World History
Iran in World History
Japan in World History
Mexico in World History
Russia in World History
The Silk Road in World History
South Africa in World History
South Asia in World History
Southeast Asia in World History
Trans-Saharan Africa in World History

Index

Abdimilkutte, 29
Abyssinians, 115
Academy, 56
Achaean League, 78
Achaemenid Dynasty, 42, 89
Adad-guppi, 40–41
Aegean refugees, 10
Aeneas, 77
Aeneid (Virgil), 76–77, 79, 90
Afghanistan, 4, 72–73, 109
Africa, 111–115, 125
  Bantu Expansion, 112–113
  caravan routes, 115–116
  Nok Culture, 113–114, 125
  sub-Saharan, xiii, 111, 113, 116
Afro-Eurasia, xi, xi–xii
  early Iron Age, 33–34
  first millennium BCE, 1–15
  second century BCE–second century CE, 87–105
  third century CE, 109
agriculture, xi–xii, xiii–xiv, 116
  in Afro-Eurasia, 91
  early Iron Age, 17
  farmlands, 47, 70
  first millennium BCE, 11, 13
  Macedonian, 54–55, 70
  mixed, 11
  in Persia, 37, 40
  small farms, 92–93
ahimsa (non-violence), 48, 67
Ahriman, 43
Ahura Mazda, 43–44
Ai Khanum, 63, 72–74
Ajatsatru, 47
Akkadian, 30
Aksum, xiii, 115
Alamanni, 119
Alashiya, 1
Alexander the Great, 57–58, 64, 125
  conquest of Persian Empire, 58–59, 66
  death of, 58–59, 64
  invasion of India, 66
  tomb, 62
Alexandria, 62–63
Almagest (Ptolemy), 63
alphabets, 20–22, 33–34
Americas, xiii–xiv
amphorae, 109
Amu Darya, 71

Amun, 10, 17, 26–27
An, 117
Anatolia, 2, 4, 64, 73–74, 125
Anavysos Kouros, 24
ancestor cults, 11
animals
  elephants, 58, 65, 67, 82, 112
  horses, xii–xiii, 11, 15, 31, 35–37, 41, 70, 81, 84
  megafauna, xiii–xiv, 29, 33, 111
  treatment of, 68
  wild or exotic animals, 64–65, 111–112, 116
Annals (Tacitus), 105
Anshan, 42
Antigonids, 59
Antioch, 118
Antiochus III, 72, 78
Antiochus IV, 62, 75
Anyang, China, 13
Apedemak, 65
Apochrypha, 75
Apollo, 25
Arabia, 30, 64–65, 90
Arabs, 76, 114
Aramaean nomads, 5, 7, 30
Aramaic, 30, 41, 59, 89
archaeology, 7–8, 11, 62–63
architecture, 63–64, 73, 105
Arch of Titus, 97
Ardashir, 118, 126
Aristarchus, 75–76
aristocracy, 65, 73, 79–80, 104, 122–123
  Gallic, 108
  hereditary, 69
  Jewish, 40
Aristotle, 46, 56, 79
Armenia, xiii, 64, 88, 123
art, 21, 64, 105, 124
  Buddhist, 100–101
  Chinese, 70
  Egyptian, 24, 27
  Gandhara-style, 121
  Greek, 24, 79–80
Artabanus IV, 118
Artemis, 25
Arthashastra, 81, 100
The Art of War (Sun-Tzu), 52
Aryans, 11–12
Arzawa, 1

Ashoka, 67–68, 125
Asian Silk Road, xii
Assur, 29
Assurbanipal, 28, 38
Assurnasirpal II, 25
Assyrian Empire, 5, 26–31, 38–39, 42, 125
astrology, 35, 64, 100
astronomy, 32, 40–41, 63–64, 100
Athenian Empire, 42, 44–46, 53–55
Attalus III, 90
Augustine, St., 121
Augustus, 88, 90, 93–95, 116, 126
Augustus of Prima Porta, 94
Aurelian, 120
autocratic monarchies, xi–xii, 59–60
Avesta, 12, 89, 123
Axumites, xi, 114

Baal Hammon, 18–19
Babylon, xi, 6, 38–39, 73, 125
  defeat by Assyrians, 27–28
  defeat by Persians, 41
Bacchae (Euripides), 89
Bacchus, 80
Bactria, 30–31, 47, 63, 71–73, 80, 85, 88–89, 98–99, 126
Bactrian coinage, 73
Bai Qi, 69
Balkans, 91
bananas, 113
Ban Chao, 116
banditry, 39–40, 79, 105, 119
Ban Gu, 89, 103–105
Bantu Expansion, 112–113
Ban Yong, 117, 121–122
Ban Zhao, 103–104
barbarians, 46, 55, 57
  Dog Barbarians (Quan Rong), 33
Barygaza (Bharuch), 110
Battle of Cannae, 77
Battle of Magnesia, 72
Battle of the Teutoburg Forest, 90
Begram treasure, 109
Bellum Punicum (Gnaeus Naevius), 77
Belsk, 37
Bel-ušezib, 35
Berber, 11
Berossus, 63
Bible, 7–8, 30, 39–40, 75
Bimbisara, 47
Bin Zhao, xii
Black Sea, 125
Blemmyes, 111
Bodhisattvas, 99–100
Book of Changes, 33
bows, 36–37, 41, 84, 102
Brahmanism, 81
Brahmins, 12, 31–32, 99
Brami, 49
bronze, 11, 16–17, 20

Bronze Age, 6, 13–15
Buddha, Gautama, 48–49, 125
Buddhism, xii, 48, 110, 121, 126
  sixth–fifth centuries BCE, 49
  fourth–second centuries BCE, 64, 67
  third–second centuries BCE, 81–82, 86
  Mahayana, 99–101, 107
buildings
  skyscrapers, 62
  temples, 45–46, 75, 79, 82

Cadiz (Gades), 18–20, 31
Caligula, 95
Cambyses, 42, 118
Canaan, 8
caravan routes, 30, 72, 115–116
caravans, 89, 109–110, 122
Carchemish, 1
Carthage, 18–20, 46, 64–65, 76–78, 106, 114
  children's cemeteries (tophets), 19
  child sacrifice, 18–19
Cassandra, 101
caste system, 12, 31–32, 47–48, 68, 99
cavalry, 35–37, 70, 84, 91, 102
  cataphracts, 120
Celtic, 47, 91
Celto-Etruscan cities, 66
Celts, 47, 66
Chaldean Dynasty, 39–40
Chandra Gupta I, 121
Chandra Gupta Maurya, 66–68, 125
Chang'an, 74, 83
chariotry, 84
China
  aristocratic tombs, 104
  Chu kingdom, 51, 82
  coinage, 51
  commanderies, 83
  dynastic histories, 88
  Eastern Han Dynasty, 126
  Eastern Zhou Dynasty, 33, 125
  education, 51–52
  fragmentation of, 122
  Han Dynasty, 51, 71, 83–84, 102–103, 116–117
  heqin or "Peace and Kinship" agreements, 85, 101–102
  imperial, 82
  intellectual life, 69–70
  Jin Dynasty, xi, 122, 126
  Later Han Dynasty, 117, 122
  Lu kingdom, 51
  patriarchal society, 87
  Qi kingdom, 51, 82
  Qin Dynasty, 51, 57, 69, 74, 82–83, 125
  regional kingdoms, 52
  relations with Rome, 116–117, 126
  reunification of, 122

146 INDEX

Shang Dynasty, 13–15, 32, 125
Shu kingdom, 122
silk trade, 50, 85, 89, 101, 110–111, 116, 122
Spring and Autumn period, 33, 50–51, 125
Sui Dynasty, 122
trade relations, 50, 70–71, 116
Warring States Period, 33, 50–51, 55, 68–70, 125
Wei kingdom, 51, 82, 122
Western Han Dynasty, 83–84, 103–104, 126
Western Zhou Dynasty, 15, 32–33, 51, 125
Wu kingdom, 122
Xia Dynasty, 13
Xiongnu wars, 102–103
Yan kingdom, 51, 82
Zhao kingdom, 51, 82
Zhou Dynasty, 32, 50, 69, 103
Chinese art, 70
Chinese literature, 33
Christianity, xii, xiii, 86, 97, 106–107, 123–124
Chuang Tzu, 69
Chu kingdom, 51, 82
Cicero, 97
Cimmerians, 35, 125
cinnamon, 111
cities, xiii, 99
  Celto-Etruscan, 66
  fortified settlements, 91, 108
  Roman-style, 92, 108
  walled, 37
Classic of Poetry, 33
Claudius, 95
Cleopatra VII, 90
climate change, xiii–xiv, 2–3, 11–12, 47
  early Iron Age, 33–34
  late Bronze Age, 15
coinage, xi, 64–65, 109
  Bactrian, 73
  in China, 51
  Gallic, 91–92
  Greek, 45
  Kushan, 100
  Lydian, 45
  Macedonian, 58, 64
  Parthian, 89
Cologne, Germany, 108
Columbus, xiv
common language *(lingua franca)*, 30, 75–76, 86
compound bows, 36–37
Confucianism, 83–84, 86–87, 105
Confucius (Master Kong), 51–52, 69, 125
Constantine, 68, 123
construction
  fortified settlements, 91, 108

skyscrapers, 62
temples, 45–46, 75, 79, 82
walled cities, 37
continental Europe, 90–91
copper, 16, 115–116
Corinth, 78
Corsica, 78
Council of Pataliputra, 68
Crassus, 89
Creation Epic, 40–41
Crete, 10, 21
crisis and recovery, 1, 4, 106–124
crossbows, 84, 102
Ctesiphon, 89
cults, 64, 97, 99–100. *See also* religion
  ancestor, 11
  devotional, 82
cultural exchange, 49, 105, 111
  culture wars, 80
  early Iron Age, 24, 29–30
  European, 90–91
  Greek, 59, 63–64, 79–80, 100–101
culture, 52, 88, 100, 121
  intellectual, 69–70, 75, 108, 124
  priestly intellectuals, 56
  scribal, 21–22, 33–34
  text-based traditions, 86
cuneiform, 30, 39, 40–41, 49, 60, 73
Cyprus, 4, 10, 16, 18, 20–21
Cyrus Cylinder, 39–40
Cyrus II, 42–44, 47, 55, 118, 125

Dacia, 111, 120
Damascus, 25
Daoism, 105
Daoists, 69, 105
Darius I, 42–44, 47, 49
David, 7–8
Dead Sea Scrolls, 75
Deccan, 99
deforestation, 17, 33
Deian League, 44
democratic government, 46, 56
democratization of metals, 16, 33–34
deserts, xii, xiii, 90, 116
Dharma (the Way), 67–68
diasporas, 97, 105
Dido, 77
Dio Cassius, 117
Diocletian, 120–121, 123–124, 126
Diodorus, 44–45
Dionysius of Halicarnassus, 98
Dionysus, 80
Diotima (website), 137
diplomacy, xii–xiii, 55, 116–117
  ambassadors, 5, 68, 118
divine authority of rulers, 105
Dog Barbarians (Quan Rong), 33
Douris (painter), 45

INDEX   147

droughts, 2–3
Druids, 91–92, 108

early Greek literature, 30
early Iron Age, 8, 16–34
east Africa, 113–115
east Asia, 13, 32
Eastern Han Dynasty, 126
eastern Mediterranean, 24, 78, 126
Eastern Zhou Dynasty, 33, 125
east–west trade, 82
eating reclining, 30
ebony, 4, 10, 49
economics, xi–xii, 52, 70, 79, 82
    food prices, 95
Edict of Milan, 123
education, 45, 51–52, 80, 121
    elite, 105
    Greek, 59, 63, 79
    philosophical schools, 56
    Roman, 108
    women's, 61, 103–104
Egypt, 114
    art, 25, 27
    conquest by Persia, 38, 42
    early first millennium BCE, 1–4, 9
    early Iron Age, 26–28
    Kushite Twenty-Fifth Dynasty, 125
    language, 65
    New Kingdom, 4–5, 8, 27, 125
    papyri, 60–61
    Ptolemaic Kingdom, 59, 62–65, 72, 125
    Syrian Wars, 72
    trade relations, 110
Egyptian, 65
Egyptian art, 24, 27
Egyptians, 97
Elam, 3, 5–6, 27–28, 38
Elamite (language), 41
Elephant Cave (Hathigumpha) inscription, 81–82
elephants, 58, 65, 67, 82, 112
elites, 60, 80, 93, 105
empire
    imperial patronage, 86, 121
    imperial rule, 66–67
    nomadic empires, 84–86, 102–103
    Roman imperialism, 90, 94–95, 120
    visual expression of, 105
Epicureanism, 63, 80
epidemics, 54, 117, 122
Esarhaddon, 28–29, 35, 38–39
Essenes, 75
Etruscans, 25, 46, 65, 95–97
eunuchs, 87
Euphrates River, 88–89
Eurasian steppe, 37
Euripides, 89
Europe, 90–91

exotic animals, 64–65, 111–112, 116
Ezekiel, 18

family life, 40–41, 69, 80
famine, 2–3
Faxian, 121
Fezzan, 116
Fiji, xiv
First Punic War, 76–78, 125
Flavian dynasty, 95
food, xii, 2–3, 95
forced labor, 40–41
fortified settlements, 37, 91, 108
Franks, 119
frontier wars, 102–103
funerary culture, 9, 11, 19, 37, 104

Gades (Cadiz), 18–20, 31
Gaius Gracchus, 95
Gaius Octavius, 93
Galatians, 66
Gallic aristocrats, 108
Gallic wars, 91–92, 108
Gandhara school of Buddhist art, xii, 121
Ganges River Valley, 47–48
Garama, 116
Garamantes, 116
Gaul, 22–25, 90–92, 108, 126
gender roles, xi–xii, 55, 61–62, 95
Geography (Ptolemy), xiv, 117
German tribes, 119
Germany, 90–92, 108, 126
Gibbon, Edward, 107–108
Gilgamesh, 38, 40–41
globalization, 14, 70, 108, 111, 117, 121–122
global warming, 2–3
Gnaeus Naevius, 77
Gnosticism, xii
gold, 36–37, 101, 111, 115–116
Gordion, 7
Goths, 119
government
    autocratic monarchies, xi–xii, 59–60
    bureaucracy, 69, 120
    clan states, 31
    constitutions, 76
    democratic, 46, 56
    by divine authority, 105
    false politicians, 56
    imperial rule, 66–67
    language of, 59, 65
    oligarchy, 54
    rule of law, 69–70
    statecraft, 81
    warrior chiefdoms, 31
Gracchi brothers, 92–93
graffiti, 22
grammar, study of, 31, 63, 81

graves
    aristocratic tombs, 104
    burial tumuli, 9, 37
    children's cemeteries (tophets), 19
Great Hunt Mosaic, 112
Great Wall, 84
Greece
    early Iron Age, 17, 22–25
    Persian invasion of, 42, 44–45, 53, 55, 125
    poleis (city-states), 20–21, 53, 56–57
    Roman, 79
    view of India, 68
Greek, 21–22, 79, 86
    lingua franca, 75–76
    simplified *(koine)*, 59
Greek art, 24, 36, 80
Greek colonies, 22–25, 125
Greek culture, 59, 63–64, 79–80, 100–101
Greek education, 59, 63, 79
Greek history, 59
"Greek-like" or Hellenistic world, 58–61, 63, 68, 75, 80, 101
Greek literature, 30, 124
Greeks, 6–7, 57, 97
    Mycenaean, 10–11
Greek warfare, 44
Gundestrup Cauldron, 91
Gupta Empire, 121

Habasha, 115
Hallstatt, 31
Hammurabi, 39
Han Chinese Empire, 51, 71, 82–86, 102–103
    divine authority of, 105
    Eastern Han Dynasty, 126
    expansion of, 102, 109
    heqin or "Peace and Kinship" agreements, 85, 101–102
    Later Han Dynasty, 117, 122
    The Records of the Grand Historian (Sima Qian), 87–88, 103
    relations with Rome, 116–117
    silk trade, 89
    Western Han Dynasty, 83–84, 103–104, 126
Hannibal, 77
Hanno, 46
Hathigumpha (Elephant Cave) inscription, 81–82
Hatti, 1
Hattusas, 4
Hazor, 3
He, 103
Hebrews, 6–8
Hellenistic period, 58–61, 63, 68, 75, 80, 101
Helots (community slaves), 55

heqin or "Peace and Kinship" policy, 85, 100–102
Herakles, 25
Herodotus, 35, 37, 41, 44, 125
Hesiod, 16, 22
hieroglyphs, 65
Himilco, 46
Himyar, 114
Hipparchus, 63–64
Histories (Herodotus), 35
historiography, ix–x, 103–104
    dynastic histories, 88
    History of the Western Han Dynasty (Ban Zhao), 103–104
    The Records of the Grand Historian (Sima Qian), 87–88
History of the Western Han Dynasty (Ban Zhao), 103–104
Hittite Empire, 3–5, 16, 26
Homer, 1, 18, 22, 79
Horace, 79–80, 97
horses, xii–xiii, 15, 35–37, 41, 70, 84
horse sacrifice, 31, 81
hostages, 102
Hou Hanshu, 117
Huan, 105
Huangdi ("Splendid Divinity") (Ying Zheng), 82–83
Iberian peninsula, 18–20, 46

I Ching, 33
Iliad (Homer), 1, 79
Illyria, 57
Immortals (Persian), 41
imperialism, 66–67
    Roman, 90, 94–95, 120
    visual expression of, 105
imperial patronage, 86, 121
incense, 30–31, 64–65, 110
India, 47–49, 80–82
    Alexander's invasion of, 66
    cities, 99
    clan states, 31
    early first millennium BCE, 2, 12–13
    early Iron Age, 31–32
    fragmentation of, 121
    imperialism, 66–67
    Indo-Europeans in, 12–13
    Maurya Empire, 67–68, 80–81, 82
    Parthian influence in, 98
    Persian expansion in, 47–49
    Shunga Dynasty, 80–82, 98, 126
    state-level societies, 13
    Varna or caste system, 12, 31–32, 47–48, 68, 99
    Vedas, 11–12, 31–32, 82
Indian literature, 99
Indian Ocean trade, xii, xiii, 49, 98–99, 110–111, 113–117, 122–123

INDEX   149

Indians, 76
Indo-Europeans, 12–13
Indo-Greek kingdoms, 81–82
Indonesia, 111
Indus Valley, 11–12, 31, 47
infrastructure, 82
intellectual culture, 69–70, 75, 108, 124
intellectuals, priestly, 56
intercontinental trade, 116
international trade, 109–110
Iran, 6–7, 17, 28, 41–42, 49, 64, 71, 89
Iranians, 12, 26, 35, 39, 72, 88
Iranian-speaking nomads, 120
Iron Age, early, 8, 16–34
iron technology, xi–xii, 31, 33–34, 51, 84
irrigation, 79, 82, 116
Isaiah, 43–44
Isis, 64, 97
Islam, xiii
Isocrates, 53, 55
Israel, 8–9, 29
Israelites, 29
Italy
    Greek emigration to, 22–25
    unification of, 92–93, 95–97
ivory, 4, 64–65

Jainism, 48–49, 81–82, 99–100
Jenne-Jeno, 113–114
Jerusalem, 8–9, 18, 39–40, 43, 74–75, 97
jewelry, 18, 21, 30–31
Jewish kingdom, 75
Jewish revolt, 62, 75, 97, 123
Jews, 30–31, 40, 43–44, 62, 73–75, 78, 88, 97
Jiang Yuan, 32
Jin Empire, xi, 122, 126
Jordan, 8–9
Josephus, 75
Judaea, 7–8, 43, 75
Judah, 8–9, 40
Judaism, 62–64, 106, 123
    Hellenistic, 75
    rabbinic, 97
Judea, 18
Judith, Book of, 75
Julia (daughter of Augustus), 93–95
Julia (granddaughter of Augustus), 93–95
Julius Caesar, 90–93, 97–98
Jupiter, 90
Juvenal, 97

Kalinga, 67, 74, 81–82
Kama Sutra, 81, 99
K'ang, 32
Kanishka the Great, 100, 126
Kartir, 123
Kaskas, 4
Kawa, 27

Kephalaia, xi
Kharoshti, 49
Kissi (Burkina Faso) 116
Kode, 1
koine (simplified Greek), 59
Krishna, 82
Kroisos, 24
Kshatriyas or warriors, 12, 31–32
Kuei-shuang tribe, 98
Kujula Kadphises, 98
Kundi, 28–29
el-Kurru, 9
Kush, 10, 26–27, 38, 49, 64–65, 80, 90, 115–116, 125
Kushan Empire, 74, 98, 126
    consolidation of, 109
    culture, 100, 121
    divine authority of, 105
    Sasanian conquest of, 121
    Twenty-Fifth Dynasty, 125
Kushites, 27, 38, 125

labor, forced or slave, 40–41, 46
Lactantius, 120
Lady Hao, 13
land redistribution, 47, 70, 103
language
    of government and trade, 59, 65
    lingua francas (common languages), 30, 75–76, 86
Laocoön, 101
Laozi, 105
lapis lazuli, 4, 30
Lapita, xiv
late Bronze Age, 13–15
La Tene, 47, 66
Later Han Dynasty, 117, 122
Latin, 79, 92, 95–98
Latin culture, 108
Latin literature, 98, 106, 124
Law Code of Hammurabi, 6
Laws (Plato), 56–57
The Laws of Manu, 81, 99
Layard, Austen Henry, 39
Legalists, 69–70
legal processes, 69, 76, 83, 123
Lessons for Women (Ban Zhao), 103–104
Levant, 17–18, 72–73
libraries, 38
Libya, 3, 9, 20
Libyan script, 116
Libyphoenicians, 20
Li Ling, 87
limes, 108–109
Linear B, 10
literacy, 21–22, 33–34
literalism, 75
literature
    Chinese, 33

classical literatures, 97–98, 105
　Greek, 30, 124
　Indian, 99
　Latin, 98, 106, 124
　oral, 21–22, 33–34
　Pahlavi, 124
　Roman, 97–98
　Sanskrit, 100
Liu Bang, 83–85, 100–101
Livy, 97
Lixus, 18–20
looting, 39–40, 79, 119
Lu kingdom, 51
Luoyang, China, 33, 116
luxury goods, 36, 70, 92, 101–102, 110, 116
　early first millennium BCE, 4
　early Iron Age, 21–25, 30–31
Lydia, 38, 42, 45–46

Macedonian kingdoms, 42, 56–70, 78–79
Magadha, 47, 66
Magi, 49
Mahabharata, 1, 31
Mahavira, 48–49, 125
Mahayana Buddhism, 99–101, 107
Mainz, Germany, 108
Mali, 113
Mamertines, 77
Mandate of Heaven, 33, 104
Manetho, 63
Mani, xi, 107, 126
Manichaeans, 107
Manichaeism, xii, 86
Marakanda, 74
Marcus Aurelius, 106, 116
Marduk, 38–40
maritime trade, 17–18, 30–31, 110, 115
Marius, 93
Master Kong (Confucius), 51–52, 69, 125
mathematics, 32, 40–41
Mathura, 99
Mauretania, 11
Maurya Empire, 67–68, 80–81
Maya, xiv
Medes, 7, 26, 39–40, 125
Mediterranean Sea, xii, 1–2, 10–11, 16–18, 20, 22, 24, 54, 78, 110, 125–126
megafauna, xiii–xiv, 29, 33, 111
Megasthenes, 68
Mei Situ Yi, 32
Melqart, 20
Memphis, 3, 114
Menander, 81–82
mercenaries, 47, 65–66, 102, 120, 123
merchants, 12, 30, 110–111, 116
Meroe, 64–65
Meroitic language, 65
Mesoamerica, xiv
Mesopotamia, 40–41, 60, 64, 71

metals
　copper, 16, 115–116
　democratization of, 16, 33–34
　gold, 36–37, 101, 111, 115–116
　iron technology, xi–xii, 31, 33–34, 51, 84
　silver, 31, 91
　tin, 16
middlemen, 12, 30, 110–111, 116
migrations, 2, 11–12, 22–25, 66, 119
　mass deportations, 29–30
Miletus, 56
military service, 69, 102–103, 123
Ming, 103
mingqi (spirit articles), 104
Mithridates VI, 90
Moab, 9
Moche, xiv
Modun, 84–85
Mohists, 51–52
molk, 18–19
monarchy
　autocratic, xi–xii, 59–60
　centralized, 68
monasteries, 99
monetization, 91–92
monks, 48
monotheism, 73–75
monsoons, 110
Monte Testaccio, 109
Morocco, 18–20
murex, 18
Mycenaean Greeks, 8, 10–11, 20–21

Nabonidus, 39–41
Nabopolassar, 39–40
Nahum, 39
Napata, 10, 114
Naqsh-i Rustam, 119
Natalism (Roman), 93–95
Native Americans, xiii–xiv
Nebuchadnezzar I, 6
Nebuchadnezzar II, 39–40
Neo-Assyrian Empire, 25–26, 28–29, 125
Neo-Babylonian Empire, 40–41
Neo-Hittites, 17–18, 27–30
nepotism, 33, 41, 80
Nero, 95
New Kingdom, 4–5, 8, 27, 125
new religions, 123–124
New Testament, 75
New World history, ix–x
Niger River, xiii, 113, 116
Nile corridor, 115
Nile Valley, 9, 115
Nimrud, 28
Nineveh, 29, 39
Nok Culture, 113–114, 125
nomadic empires, 84–86, 102–103

INDEX 151

nomads, xi–xiii, 35–37, 42, 72, 84
    Aramaean, 5, 7, 30
    early first millennium BCE, 3, 5, 7, 15
    heqin or "Peace and Kinship" agreements with, 101–102
    Iranian-speaking, 120
    steppe, 37, 50
non-violence (ahimsa), 48, 67
North America, xiii–xiv
north India, 31
Nubia, 5, 9–10, 26–28, 114
Nubian, 6–7
nuclear family, 40–41, 69

Oceania, xiii, xiv
oceans
    Atlantic Ocean, 113
    Indian Ocean trade, xii, xiii, 49, 98–99, 110–111, 113–117, 122–123
    Pacific Ocean, xiv
Odenath, 118
Odyssey (Homer), 1, 79
oecumene, xiii
Old Persian language, 41
Olmec, xiv
oppida, 91
oracle bones, 13–15
oral literature, 21–22, 33–34
Ordos Plateau, 84
Osiris, 64, 97
Ovid, 97
Oxus River, 71

Pahlavi literature, 124
Pahlavi script, 89
Palmyra, 110, 118, 120
Pañcatantra, 99
pandemics, 54, 117
Pandevas, 31
Panehsy, 5
Panini, 31
papyri, 60–61
Parni, 72
Parthenon, 53
Parthian Empire, 71–73, 88–89, 125
    divine authority of, 105
    expansion of, 73, 88, 98
    relations with Roman Empire, 88–90, 118
    Sasanian conquest of, 121
    trade relations, 89, 110, 116
Passover Seder, 30
pastoralists, 9–10
Pataliputra, 47, 67, 74, 81
Patanjali, 81
patriarchal society, 87
patronage, 81
    imperial, 86, 121
    India, 99
    royal, 81–83, 86, 104–105

Paul, 66
Pausanias, 122
Pazyryk, 37, 50, 70
"Peace and Kinship" or heqin agreements, 85, 101–102
Peleset, 8. *See also* Philistines
Peloponnesian War, 54–56, 125
Pergamum, 90
Periplus of the Erythraean Sea, 110, 126
Perpetua, Vibia, 106, 123
Persia, xi, xiii, 57
Persian Empire, 6–7, 70, 125
    Alexander's conquest of, 58–59
    invasion by Philip II, 57
    invasion of Greece, 44–45, 53, 55, 125
    rise of, 35–52
Persian Gulf, 118, 122–123
Peru, xiv
Pharisees, 75
Pharos, 62–63
Philip II, 53, 57
Philippines, xiv
Philistines, 8, 10
philosophers, 51–52, 55–56, 69–70
Phoenicia, 8, 40, 125
Phoenician, 21–22
Phoenicians, 6–7, 17–20, 23, 30
Phrygia, 26
Phrygians, 7, 35
plague, 117–118, 122
Plato, 17, 56–57, 59
Pliny the Elder, 110
polis (Greek city-state), 20–21, 53, 56–57
political order, 24, 52, 76, 122–123
Polybius, 76, 78, 82
Polynesians, xiv
Pompeii, 107
Pompeius Trogus, 98
Pompey, 93
Pontus, 90
population growth, 11, 17, 33–34, 65–66, 79, 113
Porus, 58
Prakrits, 81
Priadarsi, 67. *See also* Ashoka
priestly elites, 60
priestly intellectuals, 56
Princeps, 93
professional teachers, 51–52, 56, 104–105
Psamtek I, 38
Ptolemaic Kingdom, 59–60, 62–65, 72, 125
Ptolemy (scientist), xiv, 63–64, 117
Ptolemy I, 72
Ptolemy II, 62–63
Punic Wars, 76–78, 125
Purple People. *See* Phoenicians
Puruṣa, 12
Pushyamitra, 80–81

152 INDEX

Qi kingdom, 51, 82
Qin Empire, 51, 57, 69, 74, 82–85, 125
Qin Shihuangdi, 93
Quan Rong (Dog Barbarians), 33

rabbinic Judaism, 97
Ramayana, 31, 100
Ramses III, 1–2, 5–6, 125
rebirth, 48
The Records of the Grand Historian (Sima Qian), 87–88
Red Sea, 110, 115, 122–123
refugees, 10
Regulus, 77
reincarnation, 49
religion, xii, 64
  of the book, 86
  monasteries, 99
  monks and nuns, 48
  monotheism, 73–75
  monuments, 81–82
  new religions, 107–108, 123–124
  persecution, 123–124
  priestly elites, 60
  priestly intellectuals, 56
  state religion, 123
  tolerance, 67
  traditional Indian religion, 81–82
Report of Wenamun, 6
Republic (Plato), 56–57
Rhine River, 92
Rhine valley, 108
Rhodes, 20–21, 79
Rig Veda, 2, 12
ritual specialists, 12
roads, 49, 79, 108
The Romance of the Three Kingdoms, 122
Roman education, 108
Roman Empire, xiii, 120–123
  civil war, 90
  divine authority of, 105
  emperors, 95
  epidemics, 117
  exotic animal trade, 111–112
  expansion of, 77–80, 88, 90–93, 108–109, 118, 126
  frontier policy, 117–118
  Gallic wars, 91–92, 108
  German uprising, 90–91, 126
  Greek influence in, 79–80
  imperialism, 90, 94–95, 120
  limes, 108–109
  nucleus, 76
  relations with Aksum, 115
  relations with Carthage, 77
  relations with China, 116–117, 126
  relations with Kush, 115
  relations with Parthian Empire, 88–90, 118
  religious persecution, 123–124
  rise of, 71–86, 111, 126
  Sasanian expansion into, 118
  silk trade, 89, 116
  slavery, 80
  territory, 88, 96
  understanding of India, 68
Roman epic, 65
Roman games, 111
Roman identity, 95–97
Roman Legion, 108–109
Roman literature, 97–98
Roman Republic, 92–93
Roman Senate, 78–79, 93
Rome, xi, xiii, 65, 79–80, 95–98, 114, 117
Rosetta Stone, 61
royal patronage, 81–82, 86, 104–105
Royal Scythians, 37

Sa'ba, 30–31
sacrifice
  child, 18–19
  horse, 31, 81
Sadducees, 75
Sagala, 82
Sahara, xii, 90, 111, 113, 115–116
Sahel, xii, xiii, 116
Sais, 38
salt, 115–116
Samaria, 8–9
Samnites, 65
Samoa, xiv
Samsara, 48
Sanduarri, 28–29
Sanga order, 48
Sanskrit, 12, 81, 86, 100
Sappho, 22, 107
Sardinia, 25, 78
Sarmatians, 120
Sasanian Empire, xi, 118–119, 121, 122–124, 126
Satavahanas, 98
sati, 32
satrapies, 42, 66
scholars, 83–84, 121
schools, 45
science, 40–41, 63–64
Scipio Africanus, 77
scribes, 21–22, 33–34, 75
script, 65, 89, 116
sculpture, 24, 46
Scythian Empire, 35–38, 50
Sea Peoples, 1–2, 8, 10, 125
seas
  Black Sea, 125
  Mediterranean Sea, 24, 54, 78, 110, 125–126
  Red Sea, 110, 114–115, 122–123
  South China Sea, xii

Second Punic War, 76–78, 125
Seleucid Kingdom, 59–62, 71–72, 82, 125
　Roman victory over, 78
　Syrian Wars, 72
Seleucus (astronomer), 75–76
Seleucus I, 67-68
Seneca, xiv
Sennacherib, 38
Septimius Severus, 106
Septuagint, 63
servants or Shudras, 12, 31–32, 67
seven jewels, 110
Severi dynasty, 95
Shaka nomads, 89, 98
Shakra, 98
Shalmaneser III, 25–26
Shalmaneser V, 29
Shang Dynasty, 13–15, 32, 125
Shang Yang, 69–70
shanyu, 84, 101–102
Shapur I, 118–119, 123
Sheba, 30
Shi, 51
shipwrecks, 4, 16
Shiva, 99
Shiwei, 85
Shoshenq I, 8–9
Shudras or servants, 12, 31–32
Shu kingdom, 122
Shunga Empire, 80–82, 98, 126
Shutruk-Nahunte, 6
Sicily, 22–25, 77–78
Sidon, 18
siege technology, 28
Silis (China), xi
Silk Road, 72, 109–110, 116–117, 122–123
silk trade, 50, 85, 89, 101, 110–111, 116, 122
Silk Worm Chamber, 87
silver, 31, 91
Sima family, 122
Sima Qian, 82–85, 87–88, 102, 126
Sima Tan, 87
Sizu, 28–29
slavery, 18, 46, 60–61, 64–65, 79–80, 111, 116
　abolition of, 103
　community slaves (Helots), 55
　forced labor, 40–41
slave trade, 80, 115–116
smallpox, 117
Social War, 95
Socrates, 56, 125
Sogdians, 110
Solomon, 7–8, 18, 30
Soma, 41
Sophytos, son of Naratos, 99
Sostratus of Cnidus, 62
South America, xiii–xiv

south Asia, 11
South China Sea, xii
southern Arabia, 30
south Italy, 22–25
Spain, 31, 78
Sparta, 42, 53–55
　Peloponnesian War, 54–56, 125
Sphinx (Kawa), 27
spice trade, 30–31, 110–111
Sri Lanka, 68
star maps, 63–64
steppe nomads, 37, 50
Stoicism, 63
Strabo, 98
Strapfeet, 111
stupas, 68, 82, 99, 121
sub-Saharan Africa, xiii, 111, 113, 116
Suez canal, 49
Sui Dynasty, 122
Sulla, 93
Sun-Tzu, 52
Suppiluliama II, 4
Susa, 3, 6, 74
Syracuse, 56
Syria, 17–18
Syrian Wars, 72
Syria-Palestine, 72

Tacitus, 92, 95, 105, 108, 119
Taiwan, xiv
Tanit, 18–20
Tanzania, 114
Tarharqo, 27
Tarim Basin, 109
Tarshish, 31
Tartessus, 31
taxes, 69, 79, 103, 110
Taxila, 99
teachers, 51–52, 80
temples, 45–46, 75, 79, 82
terror, 28–29
Tethys, xiv, 127n3
Teutoburg Forest, Battle of, 90
text-based traditions, 86
textiles, 18, 21
Thales, 56
theaters, 80
Thebes, 3, 17, 53, 114
Third Century CE, 106–124
Third Macedonian War, 79
Thrace, 42, 57, 64, 91
Thucydides, 53–54
Thule, xiv, 127n4
Tiberius, 95, 106
Tiglath Pileser I, 5
Tikulti Ninurta I, 5
tin, 16
Titanius, Maes, 109–110
Titchitt Tradition, 11

Tocharian, 129n2
toleration, 67
tombs
 of Alexander the Great, 62
 aristocratic, 104
Tonga, xiv
tophets (children's cemeteries), 19
Torah, 75
trade, xii, xiii, xiv, 37, 44–45, 47, 63–66
 Arab traders, 114
 caravan routes, 30, 72, 89, 109–110, 115–116, 122
 in commodities, 109
 early first millennium BCE, 4, 8–9
 early Iron Age, 17–18, 30–31
 in exotic or wild animals, 111–112, 116
 expansion of, 70, 105, 109
 Ganges River Valley, 47–48
 Goods, xii, 71
 incense trade, 31, 64–65
 Indian Ocean trade, xii, xiii, 49, 98–99, 110–111, 113–117, 122–123
 intercontinental, 116
 international, 82, 109–110, 122–123
 land routes, 49, 75–76
 language of, 59
 in luxury goods, 4, 21–25, 30–31, 36, 70, 92, 101–102, 110
 maritime, 17–18, 30–31, 75–76, 110, 115
 Silk Road, 72, 109–110, 116–117, 122–123
 silk trade, 50, 85, 89, 101, 110–111, 116, 122
 slave, 80, 115–116
 spice trade, 30–31, 110–111
 trans-Saharan, 115–116
Trajan, 111, 118
transportation, xi–xii
trans-Saharan trade, xiii, 115–116
treaties
 "Peace and Kinship" or *heqin* agreements, 85, 101–102
 peace treaties, 55, 77
The Treatise on the Western Regions (Ban Yong), 117
tribal alliances, 37
tributes, 42, 79, 101–102
Trier, Germany, 108
Troy, 101
tumulus (burial), 9, 37
Tunisia, 18–20
Tutankhamun, 16
tyrants, 55
Tyre, 18–20, 40

Ugarit, 3
Ukraine, 37
Ulu Burun, 4, 16
upper class, 93

Urartu, 25–28, 38
urban design, 64
urbanization, xi–xii, 73, 91, 113
Uruk, 73
Utica, 18–20

Vaishyas, 12, 31–32
Valerian, 118–119
Varna system, 12, 31–32, 47–48, 68, 99
Vasudeva, 82
Vedas, 11–12, 31–32, 82
Vedism, 32
Virgil, 76–77, 79, 90, 97
Vishnu, 82, 99

walled cities, 37
Wang Mang, 103
Wang Qiang, 85
war elephants, 65, 67, 82
warfare, 50–51
 chronic, 122
 culture wars, 80
 definition of war, 79
 endemic, 92
 endless, 55
 frontier wars, 102–103
 Gallic wars, 91–92, 108
 Greek, 44
 Peloponnesian War, 54–56, 125
 Punic Wars, 76–78, 125
 siege technology, 28
 Syrian Wars, 72
 tactical innovations, 84
 Third Macedonian War, 79
 Xiongnu wars, 102–103
Warring States Period, 55, 68–70, 84
warrior chiefdoms, 31
warriors or Kshatriyas, 12, 31–32
the Way (Dharma), 67–68
weapons, 47
Wei kingdom, 51, 82, 122
welfare programs, 95
Wenamun, 5–6, 17
west Africa, 113, 125
Western Han Dynasty, 83–84, 103–104, 126
Western Zhou Dynasty, 15, 32–33, 51, 125
wheelbarrow, 84
wild animals, 64–65, 111–112, 116
wine, 101, 110–111
women, xi–xii, 22, 25, 61–62
 citizen, 21
 education of, 61, 103–104, 106–107
 Latin literature by, 106
 Lessons for Women (Ban Zhao), 103–104
 nuns, 48
 property ownership, 95
 roles for independent women, 55
 subordination of, 32, 40–41, 46, 87

INDEX 155

Works and Days (Hesiod), 16
world history, ix–x, 82
writing systems, 21–22, 33–34, 49, 86
Wu Di, 71, 87–88, 102
Wu kingdom, 122

Xenophon, 39, 55
Xerxes, 44
Xia Dynasty, 13
Xianyang, China, 83
Xiongnu Empire, 71, 84–86, 89, 101–103, 126

Yan kingdom, 51, 82
Yassthüyük, 7
Yellow Turban revolt, 105

Ying Zheng (Huangdi, "Splendid Divinity"), 82–83
Yuandi, 85
Yuezhi, 71–73, 85–86, 89, 98, 126

Zama, 77
Zanzibar, 117
Zenobia, 120
Zeus Soter ("Savior"), 62
Zhang Qian, 71–72, 75–76, 85, 126
Zhao kingdom, 51, 82
Zhou Dynasty, 32, 50, 69, 103
    Eastern Zhou Dynasty, 33, 125
    Western Zhou Dynasty, 15, 32–33, 51, 125
zodiac, 100
Zoroastrianism, xii, xiii, 43–44, 89, 123–124

Printed in the USA/Agawam, MA
November 13, 2017